Plautus: *Curculio*

BLOOMSBURY ANCIENT COMEDY COMPANIONS

Series editors: C. W. Marshall & Niall W. Slater

The Bloomsbury Ancient Comedy Companions present accessible introductions to the surviving comedies from Greece and Rome. Each volume provides an overview of the play's themes and situates it in its historical and literary contexts, recognizing that each play was intended in the first instance for performance. Volumes will be helpful for students and scholars, providing an overview of previous scholarship and offering new interpretations of ancient comedy.

Aristophanes: Frogs, C. W. Marshall
Aristophanes: Peace, Ian C. Storey
Menander: Samia, Matthew Wright
Plautus: Casina, David Christenson
Terence: Andria, Sander M. Goldberg

Plautus: *Curculio*

T. H. M. Gellar-Goad

BLOOMSBURY ACADEMIC
LONDON • NEW YORK • OXFORD • NEW DELHI • SYDNEY

BLOOMSBURY ACADEMIC
Bloomsbury Publishing Plc
50 Bedford Square, London, WC1B 3DP, UK
1385 Broadway, New York, NY 10018, USA
29 Earlsfort Terrace, Dublin 2, Ireland

BLOOMSBURY, BLOOMSBURY ACADEMIC and the Diana logo are trademarks of Bloomsbury Publishing Plc

First published in Great Britain 2021
This paperback edition published 2022

Cover design: Terry Woodley
Cover image: Roman floor mosaic from the Villa de Ruffinella, Tusculum. National Roman Museum, Rome, Italy. funkyfood London – Paul Williams / Alamy Stock Photo

A catalogue record for this book is available from the British Library.

Library of Congress Cataloging-in-Publication Data
Names: Gellar-Goad, T. H. M. (Theodore Harry McMillan), author.
Title: Plautus : Curculio / T. H. M. Gellar-Goad.
Other titles: Bloomsbury ancient comedy companions.
Description: London : Bloomsbury Academic, 2021. | Series: Bloomsbury ancient comedy companions | Includes bibliographical references and index.
Identifiers: LCCN 2020040452 (print) | LCCN 2020040453 (ebook) | ISBN 9781350079748 (hardback) | ISBN 9781350079755 (ebook) | ISBN 9781350079762 (epub)
Subjects: LCSH: Plautus, Titus Maccius. Curculio. | Latin drama (Comedy)–History and criticism.
Classification: LCC PA6568.C83 G45 2021 (print) | LCC PA6568.C83 (ebook) | DDC 872/.01—dc23
LC record available at https://lccn.loc.gov/2020040452
LC ebook record available at https://lccn.loc.gov/2020040453

ISBN: HB: 978-1-3500-7974-8
PB: 978-1-3502-1433-0
ePDF: 978-1-3500-7975-5
eBook: 978-1-3500-7976-2

Typeset by RefineCatch Limited, Bungay, Suffolk

To find out more about our authors and books visit www.bloomsbury.com and sign up for our newsletters.

for Mom and my students,
the two audiences I kept in mind
with each word I wrote

Contents

Illustrations

Figures

Tables

Acknowledgments

Top billing goes to C. W. Marshall and Niall W. Slater, for inviting me to write this book and making it better by leaps and bounds. Sharon L. James introduced me to Plautus and made me the comedy scholar I am today. Timothy J. Moore gave me the courage and tools to dive into Plautus' music and meter. I gained so much from students in my Greek & Roman Comedy course at Wake Forest University, Winston-Salem, North Carolina: insights, observations, questions, and inspiration over six iterations of the course, starting in 2013. I am especially thankful for the adaptors and performers of Plautus' *Curculio* in 2019: Brigid Berndt, Jackson Blodgett, Anna Campbell, and Cristian DeSimone. I couldn't have done any of this without the support, encouragement, and put-together-ness of Julie Pechanek. My mom, Sandra Edwards Gellar, read every word in drafts and gave invaluable feedback. Thanks also to Alice Wright, Gamey Leather, Lily Mac Mahon, Roza I. M. El-Eini, Merv Honeywood and especially Serena S. Witzke. My husband, Jake Gellar-Goad, offered his support throughout the writing, and his patience with the process—even knowing another book means I get another Classics tattoo. The bulk of the manuscript was written on ancestral lands of the Catawba, Keyauwee, Sappony, and Tutelo peoples.

I greatly appreciate Mathias Hanses, who shared a pre-publication version of his work on the Choragus with me; both he and Katrin Hanses generously allowed me to use their reconstruction of the Roman Forum in Chapter 7. I could not have completed Chapter 9 without the resources of the Archive of Performances of Greek and Roman Drama, housed at Oxford University, and the assistance of Zoë Jennings there.

I received support from the Dingledine International Faculty Fund of Wake Forest University to trace the path of the Choragus' speech in the Forum Romanum in Rome. The university's Archie Fund for the Arts and Humanities allowed me site visits to theaters active in Sicily around the time of Plautus. The university's Nathan and Julie Hatch

Research Grant for Academic Excellence sent me to the Summer Research Institute of Harris Manchester College at Oxford University. I owe thanks to Kate Wilson and Sue Killoran from Harris Manchester College, Fran Heaney and Sandra Bailey from Wadham College, Oxford University, and Elizabeth B. Dunn of Duke University, for research support. The book's completion was supported by a Wake Forest University Summer Research Award.

1

Plautus, *Curculio*, and Roman Comedy: The Basics

Imagine you're living in Rome around 195 BCE. City life is dirty, cramped, and rough. It's early April, but winter is lingering longer than usual this year. There's a biting chill every morning when you've been waking up before dawn, to show up at your boss' house for the day's work. But a break is in sight: today's the first day of the *Ludi Megalenses*, religious festival games in honor of Magna Mater, the Great Mother goddess Cybele. No business can be conducted in the City for the next seven days as the games go on.

You slept in a little later than usual this morning, but were already awake shortly after daybreak—excitement about the events to come has you feeling like a kid again. A religious festival is a public ritual, and that means free food for you and everyone else in town. You attend the sacrifice in the Forum, Rome's big public square, with thousands of other people: Romans and non-Romans, citizens and non-citizens, men and women and children, young and old, speaking Latin and Greek and Oscan and Umbrian and who knows how many other languages. The people have diverse bodies, skin, hair, and eye colors, and none of them are "white," because the Greeks and the Romans weren't white, and whiteness is a modern racial construct. It's unruly, colorful, tightly packed, and smelly.

In a few years, the Temple of Magna Mater will be complete, and the sacrifices and games will happen there instead. You faintly hear the priest's prayer to Magna Mater and all the gods from where you are in the back of the crowd. (The priest is some political bigwig from the Cornelius family, you think. They're always going on about their leadership in the long war against Carthage that ended a few years back.) You see the ritual slaughter of what seems like a whole herd of cattle, a fitting start to the festivities. And you wait with excruciating anticipation for the meat to be butchered, cooked, and distributed to everyone who's here. This is a real treat: you only eat beef at civic events like this. You can't afford it otherwise.

But the thing you're most looking forward to hasn't happened yet! Up next are the *ludi scaenici*, the theatrical performances that pulled you out of bed this morning. You hustle across the Forum towards the Comitium—where Roman citizen men vote on laws and elections, which usually turn out exactly how the elites want them to. Today, it's where the aediles (government officials who're funding the games) have set up a temporary stage made out of wood. The stage is small and flimsy, but brightly painted. It has the usual three house doors and the altar out front. You're too late to grab a good spot to sit and watch, but that's okay—what you're about to see is worth standing for.

People in the audience are still chit-chatting away, when things start up without fanfare or announcement. (Nobody turns down the lights, either, because it's ancient Rome, outdoors, and during the day, so the only lighting comes from the sun.) Two actors walk on stage, pretending to be in mid-conversation. You can tell by their Greek-style costumes that this will be a comedy, most likely an adaptation of a Greek play from Athens. And you can tell from their masks that one is playing a young citizen man and the other a trickster, enslaved to the first. You're pretty sure, from your experience, that the young guy is in love with a girl he can't have, and the enslaved guy's job will be to come up with a scheme to obtain her for him. As the noise of the crowd dies down—though not as completely as you'd like—the actor playing the enslaved character starts speaking, loudly, in the rhythmic Latin poetry that playwrights almost always use for plot exposition. The play has begun.

Something like this is what it would have been like for an average Roman to attend a play such as **Plautus**' *Curculio*, the shortest play by the Roman comedian Titus Maccius Plautus that has survived in full from the second century BCE to today. (Boldface indicates first mention of a key term, and the back of the book offers a compilation of these, as well as recommendations for further reading and notes on where I'm taking my information from.) *Curculio* is the shortest complete play from ancient Rome altogether. But it packs a lot of material into its 729 lines: sex, booze, deception, oppression, religion, law, the military, urban tourism, disease, and a long-awaited family reunion. I think *Curculio* is a perfect example of what Plautus' comedies are like generally, and at the same time an unusual play, even for Plautus.

Roman drama as a social institution

The vignette above depicts the social context for the original performances of plays like *Curculio*. All works of Roman drama, both comedy and tragedy, were usually premiered at *ludi* (public games), either as part of a religious festival or else for the funeral of a wealthy and politically powerful citizen man. This fact means that Roman plays were religious activities, as was everything else that took place at the *ludi*. That's not to say everyone had to watch in silence, filled with reverence, awe, or dread. Far from it: crowds at comedies seem to have been pretty rowdy at times, and the Romans weren't so solemn about all of their religion anyway. Plays at festivals were consecrated to the god or goddess honored by the festival, and ones performed at funeral games were part of the larger funeral ritual. The altar on the stage, the sacrificial meat in the audience members' bellies, and frequent oaths to gods in the plays' dialogue would be reminders of the religious underpinnings of the spectacle at hand. In our play, *Curculio*, religion plays a prominent role in the plot and character development (Chapter 8).

Romans celebrated a variety of religious festivals throughout the year. They didn't have weekends or even really think much about days of the week, but days when workers were generally let out for religious festivals were numerous enough that a Roman would probably have about as many days off in a year as someone nowadays working a standard office job, and festivals would offer free or cheap food and entertainment to rival a good weekend out on the town. It's unknown which festival *Curculio* premiered at, so my suggestion of the *Ludi Megalenses* (in honor of Magna Mater) is just for flavor, although evidence does survive that two other plays by Plautus were performed at particular festivals, specifically his *Pseudolus* (the *Ludi Megalenses*) and *Stichus* (the *Ludi Plebeii*).

What went on at a festival? The large, public animal sacrifices would have been quite a sight, and feasts would follow, including the sacrificial meat and more. Each festival began with a procession featuring a statue of the god or goddess the festival was for. The procession could be solemn and stately, or wild and noisy, depending on the god/dess. Usually festivals would include *ludi circenses*, chariot-races down at the *circus* (racetrack). Maybe also gladiatorial combats—generally a show of skill to first blood, not a violent battle to the death—or man-vs.-beast displays. Sideshows like acrobats and boxing weren't unheard of. People-watching had to have been part of the fun. People-*meeting*, too: **sex-laborers**, both free and enslaved, both men and women, would likely be offering their services somewhere nearby. And then there were the plays, *ludi scaenici*, "stage games."

The cost to put on these *ludi* were high, and the people in charge of paying for some festivals were the aediles, elected officials tasked with keeping Rome safe from crime and running festivals—at their own expense. It took massive wealth to go anywhere in politics in ancient Rome, either family money or maybe a loan from a friend. Being an aedile was a great stepping-stone to higher office. The aediles were divided into two groups, one with men from traditional aristocratic families (patricians) and the other with men of historically humble origins (plebeians), who, nonetheless, were rich enough nowadays to host a giant carnival out of pocket.

Being aedile opened doors to government service and provided opportunities to become famous and popular by putting on awesome *ludi*. It also meant being in charge of picking the entertainment, including the playwright and his acting troupe. The aedile may have sat in on a rehearsal or sneak-preview showing to make sure he was okay with the play. He would hire a contractor called a **choragus** to lend props and costumes to the actors, who didn't own or keep any of the stuff. The show-stealing scene of *Curculio* is the monologue of the play's Choragus (Chapter 7).

At the time of Plautus, no permanent theaters existed in the City, and they weren't allowed in for about 150 years after. So, the temporary wooden structures for performance were small and cramped. They may have incorporated a raised platform for the actors to stand on, and steps for them to get up there from the audience's level. A backdrop represented a residential street with three buildings: two houses and either a third house or, as is the case in *Curculio*, a shrine. Performers could enter the stage from the sides, from any of the three stage doors, or from the crowd. Curculio himself makes his first entrance a show-stopper by running in through the audience.

The stage for Plautus' *Pseudolus*—performed at the *Ludi Megalenses* in 191 BCE—was set up in front of the brand new Temple of Magna Mater, so that the temple steps could offer some (limited) seating. But seats weren't guaranteed. Most viewers, except the rich, the lucky, and perhaps the super-determined, could expect to stand.

The audience itself was as diverse as the City of Rome. There aren't any photos of ancient performances, obviously, or historical attendance records. So, we base our judgments on the surviving texts of comedy themselves. Plautus makes jokes and writes plots and characters that appeal to all different sorts of people: elites, poor citizens, enslaved persons, men, women, old folks, youths, parents, children, Romans, foreigners, soldiers, farmers, politicians, sex-laborers, Greek literature fans, and on, and on. His comedies are a something-for-everyone kind of show, with jokes and plotlines and characters for all of Rome's denizens in Plautus' plays. It wasn't just a diverse crowd, but a rowdy one, too. Some of Plautus' plays—though not *Curculio*—begin with a prologue. In some prologues, a guy heckles the audience and tells them to shut up and pay attention. Plautus' plays always have enough repetition of key plot points that viewers won't get lost if they're distracted every once in a while.

Roman comedy as a dramatic genre

The comedies that Plautus wrote were only one of five basic types of theater in Rome in the third and second centuries BCE. Avid theater-goers could see two types of tragedy, two types of comedy, and mime (improvisational sketch comedy acted barefoot and without masks by women as well as men, in contrast to the men-only troupes of comedy and tragedy). Roman tragedy and comedy were both divided into subgenres, depending on whether they were set in Greece or Rome, as shown in Table 1.1.

Either way, all plays were in Latin, not Greek. Exceptions: character and place names, a few words here and there, bilingual puns. Plays set in Greece were usually adaptations of Greek plays, while plays set in Rome were originals. The subgenres were named after the most emblematic costume element in each one: comedies set in Rome featured characters wearing what citizen Roman men wear, the toga, so they were *fabulae togatae*, "plays with togas." Plautus' plays, on the other hand, are ***fabulae palliatae***, "plays with the *pallium*," because his characters wear that distinctively Greek cloak. (The tragedies took their names from Greek acting-boots and the Roman magistrate's fancy *toga praetexta*.) This means that *Curculio*, like all plays by Plautus that have survived, is set in ancient Greece, with a Greek-style plot and mostly Greek characters.

Plautus and other authors of *fabulae palliatae* adapted most if not all of their plays, probably including *Curculio*, from comedies written in Greek by authors living in the Greek world. Plautus was not the first writer of Roman *fabulae palliatae*, but followed a few authors whose works have mostly vanished over time: Livius Andronicus, Rome's first playwright (about 284–205 BCE), Gnaeus Naevius, Rome's first satirist (about 270–201 BCE), and Quintus Ennius, the father of Roman literature (about

Table 1.1 Key genres of Roman drama during the time of Plautus.

	Comedy	Tragedy
Set in Greece	*fabula palliata*	*fabula cothurnata*
Set in Rome	*fabula togata*	*fabula praetexta*

239–169 BCE). For most of their source material, these authors drew on the genre of **Greek New Comedy**, written mostly after the death of Alexander the Great (late 300s throughout the 200s BCE). The only author of Greek New Comedy whose work survives in any substantial amount today is **Menander**, although fragments do remain of many other authors.

In some *fabulae palliatae*, the subgenre of Roman comedy that Plautus was writing, the prologue says what Greek play and author the Roman play is adapting. But Plautus' *Curculio* has no surviving prologue (it might have been lost somewhere along the way), so which author, or whether it's a Plautus original, is unknowable. In only one case is it possible to compare a Plautine play side by side with substantial parts of its original: Plautus' *Bacchides* ("Two Sisters Named Bacchis") and Menander's *Dis Exapaton* ("Double Trickster"). The evidence from those two plays suggests that Plautus adapted his sources fairly closely when it comes to the basics of plot and the shape of scenes, but took plenty of liberty with banter, jokes, and poetic and musical art.

Way more Roman comedy survives—in both Plautus and the slightly later author of *fabulae palliatae* **Terence** (Publius Terentius Afer)—than Greek New Comedy. A major element of twentieth-century scholarship on Roman theater was analyzing Roman practices of adaptation to try to reconstruct the lost Greek original. I think this is essentially a fool's errand, especially because it undersells how great Roman comedies themselves are. But decades of efforts by classicists committed to it have produced a thorough understanding of what's Plautine about Plautus' adaptation, and what's Roman about Roman comedy. As adaptors—for they are not merely translators—neither Plautus nor Terence allows himself to be constrained by the Greek original on any level. Both playwrights often condense or expand scenes; add, delete, or replace characters or whole scenes; and make plots simpler or more complicated. Both of them convert certain everyday features of life in Athens into analogous features of Roman life, such as turning a reference to the Agora (the Athenian marketplace) into a mention of the Forum (the public square in Rome). Similarly, they generally modify jokes that are culturally specific, so that Roman audiences can appreciate them.

But Plautus and Terence have big differences in style and in approaches to adaptation. While Terence usually keeps the character names from the original, or else just uses very bland Greek names, Plautus tends to replace them with longer, more hilarious, super-duper Greeky names. For example, a blowhard soldier in one of Terence's plays is named Thraso, a plausible Greek name that means "bold guy." But Plautus names his own blowhard soldier in *Curculio* Therapontigonus Platagidorus, a preposterous mouthful that (maybe) means "Son of a Sea Monster [or "of a Slave"], Gift of a Noisemaker." When it comes to big-picture decisions about adaptation, Terence's specialty is *contaminatio*: fusing two plays together or grafting a scene, subplot, or character(s) from one play onto another. Plautus seems to do some *contaminatio*, but not as much as Terence and not to the same degree.

Plautus as a Roman comedian

One of Plautus' hallmarks is blending elements of native Italian comic traditions into his adaptations of Greek New Comedy. The most important of these traditions was Atellan farce, a type of slapstick comedy named after a town in southern Italy (not far from Naples) where it may have originated. Atellan farce was rough-and-tumble sketch comedy, with stereotyped, clownish **stock characters**, predictable **stock plots**, and lots of improvisation and comic routines. One recurring lead character was named Maccus. This suggests that Plautus' name Maccius is probably not real but one made up to fit his profession as a funny guy. Since Titus is a generic Roman first name (plus slang for penis) and Plautus might mean "flat-footed," Mark Damen has translated Titus Maccius Plautus as "Dick Bozo Tapdancer."

Aspects of Atellan farce can be found in Plautus' plays, in certain character types that don't show up in Greek New Comedy or are less prominent there—for instance, the trickster and the not-so-humblebragger. We can also detect farce's influence in comic routines added or expanded in Plautus' adaptations. These routines include scenes where somebody pounds on someone else's door, two or three people wage a duel of insults, somebody rushes on stage to deliver a message to someone else, or two or more characters trade kicks and punches. (Those routines form a theatrical tradition, by the way, that passes from Atellan farce to Plautus to the *commedia dell'arte* of the Italian Renaissance to the Three Stooges and *Family Guy*.) In *Curculio*, in particular, the title character is a **parasite**, Greek *parasitos*, "someone who eats with you." In comedy, the parasite is a glutton who'll do anything for a free meal, especially flatter, tell jokes, and do demeaning tasks. Although parasites and flatterers show up in Greek New Comedy, the gluttony and obsession with food of Curculio himself probably takes its inspiration from another regular of Atellan farce, the ever hungry Dossennus. His big belly may also have inspired the costume of the antagonist of *Curculio*, a bloated man named Cappadox.

Much of what is distinctively Plautine about Plautus' comedies builds on the fundamental elements of Atellan farce. Greek New Comedy itself featured stock characters (young lover boy, grumpy old man, arrogant soldier) and stock plots (guy trying to get the girl, long-lost siblings reunited, mistaken identities). Plautus' adaptations closely reflect that. If you just look at plot summaries of Plautus' plays, you'll develop a good sense of what he's preserving from his Greek originals. But actually watch or read his plays and you'll find them filled with so much more, stuff you can't find on the Wikipedia page: intricate tricks and deception schemes, witty banter and wordplay, wacky stage action, disguises, sex jokes, fantastical language and imagery, misunderstandings and mockery.

These are the Plautine elements of Plautus, and they display the influence of Italian comedy more than Greek. Plautus himself seems to have been born not in Rome but in Umbria, in northern Italy. So, he was not a native speaker of Latin but of Umbrian. Therefore, he was fluent in at least three languages, since he was an Umbrian writing Latin adaptations of Greek comedies, and possibly four, since Atellan farce was originally performed in Oscan. And where Plautus' Greek originals are most interested in citizen families and marriage and legitimate children, Plautus is much more interested in enslaved tricksters; sex-laborers; puns and wordplay; twins and doubles; and song, dance, and lively stage business.

Plautus' style and language, in my opinion, are totally unique, in Latin or any other literature. He is wild and wacky, conversational yet archaic, quick to switch from dirty jokes to parody of high tragedy to lowbrow puns. He writes lots of witty banter and fast back-and-forth tomfoolery. Plautus shares some of these characteristics with the other types of comedy from his time and before, from his culture and others. His careful attention to comic style matches his Greek model Menander and his Roman successor Terence. His adventuresome sketch comedy matches Atellan farce. His fantastical wordplay and body-function jokes match the earliest genre of ancient comedy, Greek Old Comedy, whose most famous author nowadays is Aristophanes. But no other ancient author melds all these features together like Plautus does, and none of his Greek models or Roman contemporaries seems to have done it to such an extreme or with such joy and verve.

The most essential part of Plautus' style is probably his wordplay. That's also the hardest thing about Plautus to translate. Let's take an example from early in *Curculio*, lines 76–9. The young lover boy Phaedromus is talking to his enslaved attendant Palinurus about an enslaved woman next door. Try reading the Latin verse here out loud—it doesn't matter how you pronounce it, I just want you to have a feel for the patterns of sounds and mouthfuls of syllables in Plautus' words:

Ph. nomen Leaenaest, multibiba atque merobiba.
Pa. quasi tu lagoenam dicas, ubi uinum Chium
solet esse.
Ph. quid opust uerbis? uinosissima est.

Phaedromus Her name's Wildcat, she's a super-drinker and stupor-drinker.

Palinurus It sounds like you're saying "Wine Carafe," you know, like you'd put pinot noir in.

Phaedromus What else is there to say? She's winetastic.

In the space of three lines, Plautus gives us a pun and invents three new words. Leaena literally means "lioness," but Palinurus jokes that it sounds like *lagoena*, a wine jug. Phaedromus calls Leaena *multibiba*, "much-drinking," and *merobiba*, "unmixed-drinking," two **alliterative** words Plautus has coined by smashing together smaller, familiar words. After Palinurus jokes that Wildcat sounds like something you'd use to hold expensive wine from Chios, Phaedromus describes her with a novelty of a word, "super-full of wine." Plautus' plays are chock-full of this sort of inventive, fast-and-loose wordplay, and it's a challenge for translators to keep up.

Plautine humor doesn't end at wordplay, though. He creates laughs through too many techniques to cover here. Two in particular might make you uneasy, as they do me. The first is slapstick. In that same scene in *Curculio* we just looked at, the enslaver Phaedromus smacks his enslaved subordinate Palinurus any time he acts sassy, and at the end of the play, the main antagonist is roughed up by Phaedromus and his buddies (for both scenes, see the end of Chapter 3). These types of scenes are common enough in Plautus that slapstick seems to have worked for Roman audiences. The second technique unrelatable to most modern senses of humor: jokes about torture of enslaved persons. The Romans were an enslaving society. Roman wealth was built upon forced agricultural labor camps akin to the "plantations" of the American South. Roman citizens were complicit in abuses analogous to, and on the scale of, those in America during and after the colonial period. Torture of enslaved persons was a fact of life in ancient Rome. It shows up on the Roman stage, as well (Chapter 8). In Plautus, these jokes are usually made by one enslaved character to another, in the form either of "you'll get what's coming to you" or "I can take more punishment than you can."

Curculio includes a moment of this type of imagery used by one enslaved character against another. Palinurus tells Leaena, "I'd like to stab you with a cattle-prod" (131), a particularly violent fantasy perhaps pulling from his own experience of being abused. Phaedromus, who may have been the abuser, tells Palinurus to "shut up" (132), and apparently smacks him or threatens to, because Palinurus replies, "Please, don't! I'm shutting up!" (132). Phaedromus strikes Palinurus two more times in this scene (195, 196) and Palinurus laments how much he's been beaten (215).

Another feature that sets Plautus apart is his use of music (Chapter 4). Plautus' comedies are closer to modern-day musicals than to capital "t" Theater, more *Hamilton* than *Hamlet*. Over 50 percent of the lines in Plautus' plays were sung to the accompaniment of a woodwind instrument. In this, Plautus differs from the Greek New Comedy he's adapting, which had few songs besides short intermission-like interludes between units of the comedy. Almost every play of Plautus has one or many full-on song-and-dance numbers, with complex, shifting rhythms and melodic variety. *Curculio* is no exception.

Plautus reveals his other dramatic interests by how he toys with the stock plots of *fabula palliata* and by the character types that end up being stars of the show. The basic tales of Greek New Comedy are all about citizens: setting up a marriage to make citizen babies, reuniting long-lost siblings or children, resolving a crisis that affects a citizen woman's ability to produce legitimate citizen children. Roman comedy in general doesn't spend as much time on these stories—it prefers to explore the vulnerability of citizen daughters in Greek and Roman society. Plautus in particular finds those marriage stories pretty boring. He tends to use them as a backdrop for deception plots. He gives the juiciest roles not to elite citizens but to tricksters who happen to be non-citizens, enslaved persons, or non-elites. Many of his plays are named after the lead trickster, who is often a ***seruus callidus***, literally "clever slave." Our play is named this way, too, although Curculio is a low-status citizen rather than a non-citizen or enslaved person.

The tricksters come up with schemes, usually on the fly, and they always outwit their foes—their friends, too, when it comes to competitive banter. Erich Segal terms the flip-flop of social status in Plautus' plays, where enslavers and elites are bamboozled by people with less power than them, the "Saturnalian spirit" of Plautine comedy. The name comes from the Roman winter holiday Saturnalia, when enslavers would "let" enslaved people pretend to be masters for a day. Think about how twisted and cruel this is for a holiday: enslaved people are supposed to pretend to be enslavers, but they can't truly act accordingly, because the very next day everything goes back to the way it was before, and the enslavers can punish the enslaved people however they please.

Plautus also loves twins and doubles. His most famous comedy, *Menaechmi*, "The Brothers Named Menaechmus," is about a guy who comes to town looking for his long-lost identical twin and ends up in trouble with a series of people who confuse him for that very twin. (It's the basis for Shakespeare's *Comedy of Errors*.) Another Plautine comedy, *Amphitruo*, includes the first time on record that someone encounters their own double or doppelganger. Lots of scenes in Plautus use mirroring: two back-to-back speeches by different characters saying the exact same or exact opposite things. Other scenes feature duplicate sequences of action—the second on a smaller scale than the first—or one group of characters eavesdropping on a second and reiterating or refuting what they say. Part of the fun with doubles in Plautus is the fact that actors would often have been doubling roles themselves, playing two or more different characters at different points in the play.

Finally, as I see it, Plautus is the ancient playwright most interested in **metatheater** (Chapter 6). Metatheater is theater about theater. This can take the form of a play within a play, as in Shakespeare's *Hamlet*, or when one of Plautus' tricksters has a buddy put on a disguise and act like an out-of-town bigwig to pull off a heist. It can also take the form of characters talking directly to the audience or acknowledging they're characters in a play. And it shows up when characters use theater-related words as metaphors, like coming up with a "plot" to accomplish what they want or "authoring" a plan. In *Curculio*, the most prominent element of metatheater is the speech by the Choragus (Chapter 7). With his appearance, somebody who is supposed to be part of the real-life backstage crew is now coming on stage as a fictional character in order to talk directly to the audience about how their real-world surroundings are like the fictional world of the play.

Curculio as a Plautine play

The play we're focused on is a great case study for Plautus' style. It's a pretty typical Plautine plot: guy wants girl but doesn't have cash to buy her from the sex-trafficker next door. (In Roman comedy, the love interest is frequently a sex-laborer, either free or enslaved; see Chapter 2.) But the show's really about Curculio the parasite, his legendary skills at scheming and swindling, and how he faces off against both the sex-trafficker and a rival who's also going for the girl. Like many plots in Greek New Comedy and Roman *fabula palliata*, this one ends with a recognition scene—the enslaved girl is identified as a citizen, she is reunited with her family, and she's given in marriage to the guy who's been trying for her all along. *Curculio* has it all, including characteristically Plautine music and jokes and wordplay, as my earlier examples suggest.

Curculio is also remarkable for having one of almost every stock character that shows up in Roman comedy. Check out the chart of the usual suspects in Table 1.2. All we're missing is Phaedromus' mom and

Table 1.2 The principal stock types of Plautine comedy

Name	Meaning	Comments	In *Curculio*
adulescens amans	Young man in love	Technically the protagonist; usually aided by trickster	Phaedromus
seruus callidus	Clever slave	Trickster figure; often the true protagonist	Palinurus (kinda)
paedagogus	Babysitter	Enslaved guardian of the *adulescens*; tries unsuccessfully to keep him out of love	Palinurus (sorta)
seruus currens	Errand-slave in a hurry	The feckless schmuck that the *seruus callidus* plays off of	Curculio (first entrance)

parasitus	Parasite/ mooch	Sometimes just a brown-noser, sometimes a trickster, sometimes both	Curculio (rest of the play)
meretrix	Sex-laborer	Either an enslaved sex-laborer or else a free, non-citizen sex-laborer, who is often a trickster; the love object of the *adulescens*	Planesium (enslaved version)
uirgo intacta	Unwed citizen girl who's never been touched	What the enslaved sex-laborer turns out to be, implausibly	
senex	Old man	The father of the *adulescens*; Either stern and angry or horny (or both)	None
matrona	Citizen wife	The mother of the *adulescens*; the voice of reasonable conduct; sometimes an *uxor dotata*, "wife with a dowry," who dominates the relationship	None
miles gloriosus	Blowhard soldier	Also wants the love object; rival of the *adulescens*	Therapontigonus
ancilla/anus/ nutrix	Slave-girl/ old woman/ nurse	Enslaved supporting character	Leaena (anus)
cocus	Cook	Hired help; a shady character, bombastic, and kind of a klepto	Cook (unnamed)
lena/leno	Sex-trafficker	Owns or manages the love object; universally reviled	Cappadox
danista/ trapezita	Banker	Another **blocking character**; also universally reviled	Lyco

dad, otherwise it's a complete set. Palinurus and Curculio each take on two roles—doubling!—with differing degrees of success. In the play's opening scene, Palinurus switches back and forth between *paedagogus*, complaining about Phaedromus' romantic entanglement, and *seruus callidus*, making witty wisecracks at Phaedromus' expense. But Palinurus never really settles well into the role of the trickster *seruus callidus* (which in this play goes to the *parasitus* Curculio instead). Instead, Palinurus follows the lead of every other comedic *paedagogus*, by failing to keep Phaedromus on the straight and narrow. At any rate, he fades into the background after the play's early scenes. Curculio, on the other hand, makes a memorable first entrance with one of the all-time greatest *seruus currens* running scenes, despite not himself being enslaved; and he plays gluttonous parasite and scenery-chewing trickster with equal perfection for the remainder of the play. All of the other characters in *Curculio* play exactly to type (except the sex-trafficker Cappadox: Chapter 8).

What was the original play of Greek New Comedy that Plautus was adapting into *Curculio*? Plautus doesn't tell us, so we can't know what it was. Questions about the play's relationship to its original, though worth consideration, must remain shrouded in uncertainty, and ultimately in my view are not the most interesting or important aspects of studying *Curculio*. We can't tell whether he was even working from an original, or just writing a brand new play in the style and tradition of his genre, as Eckard Lefèvre suggests. A key sign of Plautus' heavy adaptation of the original is the play's length. No surviving play of Greek New Comedy appears to have been as short as *Curculio*—presuming, of course, that *Curculio* has survived to the present day without big chunks going missing. One potential motivation for Plautus' abridgement is that the aediles who paid him to produce *Curculio* wanted him to keep it short. Alternatively, Plautus could've been removing what he thought of as dull fluff, to make room for improvised jokes and extensive monkey business that fills up time on stage without filling up lines on the page. Some features of *Curculio* can be interpreted as signs of compression of his Greek original, as Elaine Fantham discusses. No prologue explains what's going to happen, though this is common in Menander. (The Greeks and Romans seemed to have wanted spoilers.) Meanwhile, Curculio's pivotal trickery of Therapontigonus is relegated to a backstory rather than taking place in front of our eyes. And *Curculio* lacks a scene where Therapontigonus recognizes Curculio and realizes he's been had, but instead includes merely a single line from him in a monologue.

The most obvious element of Plautus' originality in *Curculio* is the speech of the Choragus. Simply put, nothing else like it exists anywhere in surviving Greek New Comedy and Roman comedy. It goes against an unwritten rule of the genre: never do specific, political, present-day jokes. We have no parallels for anything like this scene in Terence or in what today remains of Menander. The Choragus as stage official does not exist in the Greek theatrical tradition. And the Choragus' speech is like Plautus himself—built on a Greek foundation, but thoroughly Roman, completely embedded in the City of Rome, and totally in sync with everyday life.

In the next two chapters, we dive into the play's plot, themes, and sources of humor. Then, Chapters 4 and 5 will give a feel for what *Curculio* was like in performance, with music, costumes, props, and stagecraft. Chapters 6 through 8 cover important issues in this play: first, metatheater; next, the Choragus; then, how *Curculio* illustrates the real lives of Romans in the areas of sex, enslavement, religion, food, and poverty. Chapter 9 connects the dots from then to now, tracing how *Curculio* made it into the modern world, and how the modern world has re-made *Curculio*.

2

What's Going on in *Curculio*?

In this chapter, we begin with a summary of *Curculio* from the perspective of the audience watching it unfold. Then I'll turn to three of the play's major building blocks: a "love" story, a deception, and a family reunion.

Two characters come on stage in mid-conversation. The first person to speak is an enslaved man, as indicated by his mask (Chapter 5). His opening lines: "Where should I say you're headed outdoors tonight with that getup and this entourage, Phaedromus?" (lines 1–2). This tells the audience to imagine a nighttime scene; provides the name of the young citizen man being questioned; and draws attention to the line of silent characters, all enslaved to Phaedromus, who follow him. (It will be several minutes before anyone says the name of the person who asked the question: Palinurus.)

Phaedromus answers, "Where Venus and Cupid order me to go, where Love encourages me to" (3). Venus is goddess of love, Cupid her son, the mischievous god of desire: it's a love story, or something close to one. When Roman comedies begin with a young man announcing his infatuation with somebody, it's usually for a young woman he cannot have. (Don't think that ancient comedy is totally hetero, though. Men in Greek and Roman comedy express sexual attraction to other men with some frequency: Aristophanes' plays are full of it, and scenes with clear homoerotic innuendo or expressions of homoerotic desire appear in Plautus' *Asinaria* and *Casina* as well as Terence's *Eunuchus*. The men who wrote most of surviving Graeco-Roman literature generally kept silent about women's homoeroticism.) Either the young woman is enslaved to a sex-trafficker and he cannot afford to buy her for himself, or she's a free sex-laborer and he cannot afford to buy exclusive access to her. Generally, in these kinds of tales, the lover boy (*adulescens amans*) will scrounge up the cash via his enslaved attendant, who will swindle the sex-trafficker or the lover boy's dad.

Palinurus and Phaedromus continue their conversation (14), indicating that the building between Phaedromus' house and the house they're going to is a shrine to Aesculapius, god of healing, whose most famous religious site is the Greek city of Epidaurus. Perhaps that's where this play is set! Phaedromus leads Palinurus and the rest of the procession past the shrine and then does something odd: he says hi to the door of the house he's been walking to (17). Palinurus makes fun of him—seems like Palinurus is turning out to be a *seruus callidus*.

But once he figures out Phaedromus has gone out at midnight to see about a girl, Palinurus goes off on a rant about how Phaedromus needs to avoid sleeping around with citizen women (27–38). Maybe Palinurus is supposed to be the stern, moralizing *paedagogus* instead? Anyway, Phaedromus quickly reassures Palinurus: the house belongs to a sex-trafficker (*leno*, 39), and Phaedromus has fallen for one of the girls enslaved to him. He claims the feeling's mutual. He mentions that the sex-trafficker is sick, bad enough to visit the shrine next door overnight in hopes that Aesculapius will help him recover (61–2). The sex-trafficker is saying Phaedromus will have to pay a high price if he wants to buy his beloved sex-laborer. But, of course, Phaedromus, like all citizen lover boys in these plays, has no cash, so he's sent his parasite overseas to try to procure a loan (67–9). (It goes unexplained how he can afford to send someone overseas if he has no cash, but these kinds of inconsistencies are common enough in Plautus' comedies.) Yet, if the parasite is taking care of Phaedromus' cash problem, then Palinurus probably won't have much to do with the tricks and schemes—no *seruus callidus* in this play.

Phaedromus continues being weird with the door: he sprinkles some wine at its threshold, as if making an offering to a god, and talks to it some more (79–89). Out comes an old woman, who's caught the scent of wine and has gone wild for it (96–109). This one in particular is

Leaena, the winetastic Wildcat. Leaena doesn't speak, though—she sings. She sings about wine, she receives wine, she drinks wine eagerly, she cracks jokes about wine, then she goes inside to bring out the girl Phaedromus has come to see. As she does, Phaedromus once again talks to the door, this time with a song of his own, a weird hymn or magical spell, which is also a paraclausithyron (a song sung by a lover in front of a beloved's door, 147–57; Chapter 4).

Leaena leads out the sex-laborer—her mask is that of a beautiful young girl, as expected—and at last her name is spoken, Planesium ("Little Wanderer," a fitting moniker for a survivor of human trafficking.) Phaedromus and Planesium banter and embrace, Palinurus and Planesium exchange insults, and Phaedromus smacks Palinurus around (162–202). Then the door to the shrine of Aesculapius opens (203), so the lovers go their separate ways back into their separate houses, Planesium accompanied by Leaena and Phaedromus by Palinurus. On his way out, Phaedromus promises to free Planesium within three days (208–9).

The stage is empty for only a moment before someone exits the shrine. The actor's mask indicates that it's the sex-trafficker, but he looks odd, and he's coming from the wrong door. The red skin tone of masks depicting men is for this guy a bit greenish, and his costume includes a grotesquely puffed-out belly. He's moaning, apparently very sick. He delivers a short monologue about how his illness is a sign Aesculapius dislikes him (215–22).

Palinurus comes out of his house while giving some romantic advice to Phaedromus (223–8). Palinurus sees the sex-trafficker—Palinurus helpfully says his name is Cappadox ("man from Cappadocia," in modern-day Turkey)—and they banter. Then Cappadox asks Palinurus to interpret a dream he just had in the shrine (245–7). Before Palinurus can begin, yet another character emerges from Phaedromus' house, this time a cook (251). He takes over from Palinurus, sends him inside, and gives Cappadox a rather obvious interpretation of the dream: if Aesculapius was avoiding Cappadox in the dream, he must find a way to placate the god (260–72). Cappadox and the Cook each go back inside, leaving the stage empty once more (273).

Palinurus comes back out and says he sees Phaedromus' parasite returning home. He calls Phaedromus out. The two of them move off to the side to watch the parasite's entrance (274–9).

Here's where things turn wild.

A ruckus breaks out at the back of the crowd. It's the parasite! He's actually in the crowd! He's shouting, pushing people aside, moving fast without really going very far. As he makes his way towards the stage, he goes on a tirade about how he's too busy to have time for anyone, no matter how rich or powerful (280–98). Phaedromus approaches him and calls him by name: Curculio. They catch up with one another, and all the while Curculio complains about how hungry and sick of travel he is. Phaedromus turns the conversation to the loan he needs. Curculio dashes his hopes for cash—but says he has a plan (335).

While he was off in Caria (also in modern-day Turkey), he says, he met a soldier who said he'd contracted to buy a girl from Cappadox and had placed money on deposit with the banker Lyco (336–48). The soldier said Lyco would give it to whoever came to Epidaurus bearing the soldier's signet ring. (The inference that the play was set in Epidaurus is correct, 300-plus lines later.) The soldier then invited Curculio out for some wine and a game of dice. As they played, the soldier invoked Planesium's name for good luck (336)—so, Curculio's story shows the soldier is Phaedromus' rival! Curculio kept drinking and dicing until the soldier passed out, at which point Curculio stole his signet ring and hightailed it out of there (360–3).

After telling this improbable story, Curculio heads inside with Phaedromus to forge some documents (but only after Curculio talks some more about food). Someone comes along the road, talking about banking: this must be Lyco. After a few lines from him (371–83), Curculio emerges again, but with an eyepatch on. (In a few moments, he'll give a fake name, "Summanus.") The banker—he apparently doesn't recognize Curculio, either because of the disguise or maybe because they've never met before—makes fun of Curculio's apparent disability. The two argue for a bit, until Curculio turns to business, passing off the fake documents with some lies thrown in for good measure (392–454).

During their conversation, they mention the name of the soldier, Therapontigonus Platagidorus, a preposterously Greek, preposterously long name that Lyco mocks.

Cappadox enters and joins Lyco and Curculio in conversation (455). He doesn't recognize Curculio, either. Lyco tells him to send Planesium along with Curculio. Cappadox mentions he's sworn an oath to hand her over only to the soldier, but Lyco persuades him to ignore the oath. That's typical behavior for comedy's sex-traffickers: perjury and oathbreaking are their favorite pastimes. All three enter Cappadox' house to finalize the transaction (461).

Then something happens unlike anything comedy fans living in Rome have ever seen. Someone comes onstage dressed like a Roman, not a Greek, talking about how wily Curculio is and how he might not recover the costumes he's lent to Curculio. This is meant to be the play's choragus. He promises to show the audience where to find good guys and scoundrels throughout the City—Rome, not Epidaurus—and then goes on a kind of verbal tour of the Forum, right where the play is taking place (467–86). From where he's standing, he points out different areas nearby and says which types of scumbags like to hang out in each spot.

The crowd is loving it. After he's hit all the most famous places, from the Old Shops down to the Etruscan Quarter, he heads backstage.

And then the play continues like normal: Cappadox, Lyco, and Curculio (still in disguise as "Summanus") re-emerge with Planesium in tow (487). Lyco and Curculio take turns reminding Cappadox of his oath. Curculio rants about the corruption of sex-traffickers and bankers. Possession of Planesium is formally transferred to Curculio. She exits with him, and Cappadox and Lyco part ways (524–32).

A new character bursts on stage. His sword and cloak identify him as a soldier—Therapontigonus Platagidorus himself. He's raging at Lyco, who's following after him (533–54). They're arguing about money. When Lyco mentions "Summanus" as Therapontigonus' agent, the soldier is bewildered, and Lyco leaves. Cappadox then enters (557), and Therapontigonus tells him to hand over Planesium. But Cappadox, too, mentions "Summanus," and Therapontigonus finally realizes he's been tricked by Curculio. Cappadox leaves the soldier perplexed and frustrated (588–90).

Things are moving quickly now, the action is picking up and moving towards a climax. Curculio returns, complaining that Planesium is showing too much interest in his ring, the one he stole from the soldier when they were overseas (591–8). Planesium and Phaedromus hurry after him. She's insisting they catch up and examine the ring—and then she drops a big new piece of information. She was, she says, born free (607).

At this point, Therapontigonus joins the conversation and demands Planesium (610–15). She presses Phaedromus to ask Therapontigonus where he obtained the ring Curculio stole. He says he was given it by his dad. Planesium recognizes the symbol on the ring as her father's seal—and so recognizes Therapontigonus as her long-lost brother! She gives him enough information on her backstory to convince him she's truly his sister (641–57). Curculio prompts Therapontigonus to approve of Planesium marrying Phaedromus. Since their father is gone, Therapontigonus alone has the legal power to arrange the marriage.

The big reveal and reunion have taken place, lover boy's gotten the girl, a wedding's in the near future. All that's left is to punish the sex-trafficker, and that's what happens for the final ten minutes or so of the show. Cappadox comes on, and the rest of the characters mess with him (679–728)—although Planesium does intercede on his behalf, asking them not to be too rough, because he was not unkind to her. They force him to pay Therapontigonus back. Then the cast asks for applause (729), signaling the end of the play.

Plot points—Part one: Love is just a four-letter word

It's pretty typical for plays by Plautus, for other plays in this genre, and for plays in the genre of Greek New Comedy that Plautus adapts all to feature a young citizen man infatuated with a girl or young woman he's having trouble gaining access to. Between a third and a half of Plautus' surviving plays do this. Sometimes, it's because she's a sex-laborer and he can't afford to pay her. Rarely, it's a freeborn girl he wants to marry but can't persuade her father (or his own) to agree. Often, as in *Curculio*, it's because she's enslaved and he cannot afford to purchase her for himself or buy her freedom from the sex-trafficker. (The purchase price in this play—30 *minae*, mentioned at 63, 344, 492, 535, and 666—is the standard price for a girl in Plautus' comedy, and extremely expensive, approximately ten years' pay for a construction worker.)

So, is this play—or at least the parts focused on Planesium and Phaedromus—a love story? Consider the evidence on each side. First, in favor. The play opens with Phaedromus talking about offerings to Venus, the Roman goddess of love and sex. The two young characters seem smitten with one another in their first meeting on stage (163–214). Even before that, Phaedromus is confident that Planesium has totally fallen for him ("she loves me to death," 46). The moment Phaedromus realizes at the end of the play that Planesium is a freeborn girl, he's immediately ready and waiting to marry her, and when Therapontigonus leaves the marriage question up to Planesium, she says she wants to.

But the Romans weren't really about "true love." The point of marriage in ancient Rome was to form political, social, or economic alliances and to ensure the production of citizen children. This basically holds true for the Greeks whose comedies Plautus was adapting, too. Phaedromus' interest in Planesium developed before she was identified as a freeborn citizen girl, and so he certainly wasn't initially thinking of her as a potential wife. We should also keep in mind that Planesium was enslaved to a sex-trafficker: isn't it likely that Phaedromus first met Planesium on a visit to Cappadox' house, in effect a brothel, or at least a showroom for sex-slaves? Phaedromus was probably on a sex-shopping trip.

So, Phaedromus could be suspected of entering this relationship from a position of erotic infatuation, not romantic affection. For circumstantial evidence, we can also add the unbalanced exchange of sentiments he initially describes between her and himself: "she loves me to death; I, on the other hand, don't want to share her with anybody" (46–7). This sounds less like reciprocal romance and more like a guy with an inflated ego who wants his chosen sex object all to himself and is sure she feels that way, too. Granted, he subsequently says, "I love her just as much, as well" (48), but his clarification comes up only in response to a follow-up question, and so his headline is bound to be the sexually greedy rejection of anything but an exclusive relationship with Planesium. Phaedromus similarly does tell Palinurus early in the play that he and Planesium have done no more than kiss (51–2). But this detail is included mostly to make clear to the audience that Planesium has not yet had sex with anyone and so can still qualify as a *uirgo intacta* (see Table 1.1 in Chapter 1), eligible for marriage upon liberation from slavery.

Lover boys in Roman comedy often go through a phase where they have fun with free or enslaved sex-laborers, with the expectation that someday they'll finally grow up and start acting like real men by getting married. This is how I think we should view Phaedromus at the opening of the play. He's a horny young guy, looking to obtain a sex object during the no-strings-attached stage of his misspent youth. Only by chance does it turn out that the girl he wants is what his society considers to be marriage material, and so it's only by chance that Phaedromus leapfrogs his way into responsible, married adulthood by play's end.

We can also observe the erotic calculus Phaedromus faces in an exchange he has with Palinurus (25–38):

Palinurus Tell me you aren't planning an ambush against some chaste girl, or a girl who oughtta be chaste?

Phaedromus Of course not, and may Jupiter never allow me to!

Palinurus That's how I feel, too. If you're smart, arrange it so you always have sex with what's yours, so that if people find out what you're having sex with, you'll look above-board. Always be careful you don't end up intestate [*intestabilis*].

Phaedromus Wait, what does *that* mean?

Palinurus That you should follow the path cautiously: whatever you have sex with, do it with your testes [*testibus*] intact.

Phaedromus But c'mon, a *flesh-peddler* lives here.

Palinurus Well, nobody forbids or blocks you from buying what's openly for sale, if you've got the cash. Nobody blocks anybody from walking on a public street. As long as you don't blaze a trail through private property, as long as you keep away from married women, widows, citizen girls, young men, citizen boys—have sex with whoever you want.

Palinurus warns Phaedromus against taking an erotic interest in freeborn people, whether married, unmarried, or widowed, woman or man. (He also makes a nice pun on the Latin word for "witness," *testis*: only men could bear witness, and testicles were considered one of men's distinguishing features, while in ancient Rome, castration was a possible punishment for violating the rules of sexual conduct described in these lines.) By contrast, Palinurus endorses erotic interest in people to whom sexual access can be bought or who can themselves be sold. Palinurus' moralizing rests on the assumption that Phaedromus hasn't left the house in the middle of the night in search of a wife, but rather a good lay.

In giving sexual advice to the young man he's enslaved to, Palinurus takes on the role of erotodidact, "teacher of love/sex." Think of Cyrano de Bergerac, or the iconic scene in sitcoms and romantic comedies where a nerdy guy is on a first date and his smooth-talking buddy feeds him lines through an earpiece—those are classic examples of erotodidaxis. So is dating advice, or guides in men's magazines about sex techniques, and (in more toxic forms) "Pick-Up Artist" websites and "locker-room talk."

In *Curculio*, Palinurus' pose as erotodidact comes out not only in his explanations of the kinds of sex objects Phaedromus should avoid or should seek, but also in his objectification of those objects. He repeatedly uses the neuter forms of words in reference to them (e.g., *id quod*, "that which," 29; similarly, 31, 34, 38) instead of masculine or feminine forms. He even compares a sex-slave to public infrastructure ("nobody blocks anybody from walking on a public street," 35). But his teaching of the ways of love ends up being pretty tame. Unlike erotodidacts in Plautus' successors (the enslaved assistant Parmeno in Terence's play *Eunuchus*;

the narrator of Ovid's satiric poem *Ars Amatoria*, "the Handbook for Getting Laid"), Palinurus warns Phaedromus away from sexual assault (23–6), especially by expressing concerns about an "ambush" (25) Phaedromus might be planning against his sex object of the moment. His rules at the end of the passage—don't sleep with a citizen woman who's not your wife, don't sleep with young citizen men or citizen boys (37–8)—in fact describe the basic, traditional code for elite Roman citizen men's sexuality.

What about Planesium? At each step of the way she is facing a life of sex-slavery. We shouldn't underrate the coercive power of her circumstances. If Cappadox can't sell her, he might consign her to brothel enslavement or streetwalking prostitution, two of the most brutal fates conceivable in the ancient world. So, it is in her utmost best interests to find a man interested in buying her and able to afford it. This alone could explain her performance of affection for Phaedromus in her early scene: maximizing the chances that he will fall for her hard enough that he'll scrounge up the money to buy her off Cappadox. She could just be doing her job: as an enslaved sex-laborer, pleasing her enslaver entails attracting and snagging paying clients.

Later, once she's been recognized as free, she is indeed given the choice to marry Phaedromus or not. But here, too, it isn't clear-cut. As an unmarried citizen girl, Planesium knows her brother Therapontigonus will eventually arrange a marriage for her. With Phaedromus, she at least has a somewhat-known quantity, and someone of roughly the same age.

An unusual feature of *Curculio* among Plautus' comedies is the absence of citizen parents. Phaedromus' mom and dad are nowhere to be found. In other plays, one or both parents might be an antagonist, or might themselves be stars of the show. Their absence means Phaedromus has no role models within the play for married life, and more importantly has no father around to formally (and legally) approve the marriage to Planesium. In Roman elite thinking, young men weren't fully adults until around age 30, and could be subject to their fathers' authority until marriage or even until the father's death.

In *Curculio* we only have comparative evidence—how marriage plots go down in other plays by Plautus and Terence and Menander—to tell us that Phaedromus' wedding will be okay with his dad, who ultimately would make the decision. The absence of Phaedromus' parents is, I think, more about keeping the focus on Curculio and on the recognition plot (the rest of this chapter) than it is a thematic message. Or maybe instead we should be disquieted about the missing parents, and in the back of our minds question the legitimacy of the marriage agreed to at play's end, and worry about how Phaedromus will treat Planesium since his own parents are truants (or dead?).

Finally, Phaedromus' erotic rival for Planesium, Therapontigonus, ends up being her brother. If Curculio's schemes hadn't worked, Therapontigonus would have purchased his own sister as his sex-slave: near-miss incest. This is uncomfortable, for Romans and even for Greeks, and it would be a surprise for the audience. If we pay close attention, we can find a hint of it early on in the play, when Phaedromus is telling Palinurus how he and Planesium haven't yet had sex: "she's had as little sexual contact with me as if she were my *sister*, unless kissing counts as her being unchaste" (51–2). This isn't the only near-miss incest in Plautus; it nearly happens between two half-siblings in his play *Epidicus*. But, if you're shocked, watch *Star Wars: The Empire Strikes Back* (1981), and you'll see a sensual, eager kiss between Luke Skywalker and Leia Organa, revealed as siblings in the next movie.

Plot points—Part two: Turning trickster

In *Curculio*, the title character takes on the role of trickster. In other plays of Plautus, the trickster is often an enslaved person (for example, the title characters of *Pseudolus* and *Epidicus*, Chrysalus in *Bacchides*, Pardalisca in *Casina*) or a free sex-laborer (such as Phronesium in *Truculentus* or the titular twin sisters of *Bacchides*). Only here and in Terence's *Phormio* among surviving comedies of this genre is the lead trickster a parasite—and *Phormio* is influenced by *Curculio* (Chapter 9).

When the trickster's a man and the cast list includes a lover boy like Phaedromus, the trickster's tricks are usually intended to help lover boy get the girl: in this case, to help Phaedromus obtain the cash he needs to buy Planesium. Before the time of the play itself, Curculio's marching orders were innocent enough: simply a journey to Caria to hunt for a loan on Phaedromus' account (67–8). Though he comes up short on his mission, he's in the perfect position to salvage the situation when he encounters Therapontigonus. By a fantastical coincidence of the sort that only happens in comedies, the soldier has business with Phaedromus' neighbor Cappadox and local banker Lyco, and has a financial stake in none other than Planesium herself. Soldiers in comedy—unlike lover boys—are loaded with cash, so Therapontigonus instantly reads like the perfect target for Curculio. The parasite proceeds to do what he does best: score an invite to hang with Therapontigonus at the soldier's expense (349–52). Chatting leads to dice, dicing leads to drinking, and once Therapontigonus is good and drunk, Curculio shifts gear from parasite to trickster and steals the soldier's signet ring.

Therapontigonus tells the parasite that he's arranged with the banker to give Therapontigonus' cash to whoever comes with tablets sealed by Therapontigonus' insignia (345–8). So when Curculio takes the ring, he already knows what he's going to do with it: forge a letter purporting to be from Therapontigonus and seal it with the ring to give it false credibility (365). The ring—the soldier's proof of identity—is a magic key that allows Curculio to thwart Lyco the banker and Cappadox the sex-trafficker, the two formidable blocking characters who stand between Phaedromus and Planesium.

The next step after forging the documents is to put them to use. Since Curculio lives in Epidaurus, same as the two guys he needs to trick, he plays it safe and puts on a disguise, an eyepatch. (If you think a simple change in eyewear isn't plausible enough to conceal a fictitious character's identity, file a complaint with Clark Kent.) He pretends to be a freedman of Therapontigonus. In Roman tradition, once a formerly enslaved person had been released from servitude by the enslaver, the newly free still owed allegiance to their former master, so the soldier's freedman is a believable candidate to be his agent in buying Planesium. Curculio adopts the fake name "Summanus" and successfully fools both Lyco and Cappadox in order to take possession of Planesium (371–461, 487–532). The proof that Curculio's deception scheme goes off without a hitch is that first Lyco (522, 533–54) and then Cappadox (557–82) call Curculio "Summanus." It's only after Therapontigonus has heard about "Summanus" from those two that he realizes Curculio is to blame for his loss of Planesium (583–4).

Curculio manages the pivotal deception plot with skill and ease. He also brings a commanding presence to every scene he's a part of while the tricks are still afoot. Most notable, of course, is his grand first entrance, probably coming in through the audience and delivering a virtuoso version of the *seruus currens* "errand-slave" monologue. When he's reporting the results of his journey to Phaedromus, he plays up the suspense, for Phaedromus and the audience both, by drawing out his story about meeting and cheating the soldier (328–70).

Later, when hoodwinking Lyco, Curculio has to play the part of the boastful soldier's lackey persuasively. He does so by listing a preposterous number of real and fake territories he says Therapontigonus conquered (442–8):

> He singlehandedly, in under twenty days, conquered the Persians, Paphlagonians, the people of Sinope, the Arabs, Carians, Cretans, Syrians, Rhodes and Lycia, Hunger-y and Wine Country, Centaurbattalia and Fleetland, Singleboobistan and Libya, the whole Brownnosian coast, half of all peoples everywhere.

Overblown, preposterous claims of military might are a standard characteristic of comedy's soldiers and their sidekicks, so Curculio is pitch-perfect with this run-on sentence. And Lyco buys it hook, line, and sinker, telling Curculio, "damn, you're spewing out so much nonsense that I totally believe you came from" Therapontigonus (452). Curculio, playing the gopher of the *miles gloriosus* (blowhard soldier) in order to pull off his ultimate trick, succeeds in being *gloriosus* (blowhard) enough to fit the bill.

Plot points—Part three: Recognition and reunion

Let's pause for a moment to admire the economy of plot in this play: the "love" story hinges on the deception plot, and the deception plot leads directly to the third big story element in *Curculio*, the reunion of long-lost siblings Planesium and Therapontigonus. In writing this play, Plautus has tied together three classic stock plots of Roman comedy into a neat bundle. Curculio's motivation for tricking the soldier, the banker, and the sex-trafficker is to grant Phaedromus access to the object of his erotic infatuation. At the same time, his main tool for pulling off the heist—the soldier's ring—becomes the way Planesium recognizes she's the soldier's sister and therefore undeniably freeborn. And that identification wraps back around to conclude the love story with a not-so-unpredictable twist, the engagement of Planesium and Phaedromus to be married.

Recognition scenes are so fundamental to Greek and Roman theater that they have a technical term we take from Greek: anagnorisis. In comedy, it's usually recognizing a long-lost family member or discovering someone's identity in a way that allows for marriage between young citizen woman and young citizen man. Sometimes, it's just figuring out that identical twins are roaming the neighborhood. In *Curculio*, we find both types of comic recognition combined into one. Planesium and Therapontigonus are reunited as sister and brother. This turn of events simultaneously removes Therapontigonus as Phaedromus' erotic rival, makes Planesium eligible for marriage to him, and accords Therapontigonus the authority to approve said marriage. Comic recognition scenes often depend on some sort of token—baby toys from a long-lost child, a brooch or ring wrested from an assailant during a sexual assault, an heirloom. For *Curculio* it is the signet ring belonging to Therapontigonus, a gift from his father. Planesium's father had a ring just like it, she recalls. If Curculio hadn't stolen it from the soldier as part of his scheme to get the girl, he wouldn't have been wearing it when in Phaedromus' house after bringing Planesium there, and she wouldn't have seen it and recognized it (the first stage in the play's recognition).

But maybe this means that Curculio's whole scheme didn't really matter in the big picture. If he hadn't stolen the ring, Therapontigonus would still have it and would buy Planesium without difficulty. She would then see the ring when brought to his household as an enslaved sex-laborer, and the reunion would happen there (but maybe only after incest had occurred).

Regardless, the recognition/reunion plot touches on an anxiety that might have been a common experience among the members of the audience for *Curculio*. For almost an entire generation during the time of Plautus' plays, the Romans were engaged in the second and most total of their wars with the Phoenicians of Carthage. During the Second Punic War, the Carthaginian general Hannibal crossed the Alps, invaded Italy, and soundly defeated Roman armies a number of times before being pushed back. The average person living in Rome likely would have known someone who did a tour of duty in the fighting; a lot of those soldiers didn't come back. Families in this period could easily have been torn apart. Long-lost relatives returning—or never being heard from again—were part of real life, not just sensational plot points on stage. And human trafficking intensified during Rome's military expeditions and growing imperialism. The story of Planesium and Therapontigonus could hit close to home for audiences in Rome, could act out some of their unfulfilled desires, could help them grapple with their greatest heartbreaks.

3

Major Themes and Humor in *Curculio*

Besides the big chunks of the storyline, some recurrent motifs in our play are worth noting. A big one, religion, connects in part to the play's setting, Epidaurus, a central site for the worship of the healing god Aesculapius (Chapter 8). Let's survey three other themes: animals, commerce and law, and sickness.

Animals

The animal theme begins with the title of the play itself. A *curculio* in Latin is a weevil, a kind of beetle that likes to hang out in grain storage and eat through the stockpiles (Figure 3.1). This is a fitting name for the most superb of Plautus' parasite characters. Plautus jokes on Curculio's name near the end of the play: Therapontigonus asks Cappadox, "where can I find Curculio now?" (586). Cappadox responds with some sass: "Easy!: in a grain-heap, I can guarantee you'll find not just one but fifty curculios!" (586–7).

Leaena, the old door-keeper at the house of Cappadox, is "Lioness"/ Wildcat. She behaves more like a bloodhound, though. Phaedromus informs Palinurus that she'll recognize him from the smell of a few drops of wine (80–1). In her first line of dialogue, Leaena says her nose has caught scent of that wine (96), and she claims that wine's odor makes all other fragrances smell like what tanners use to strip hair off oxhides (101), that wine is for her the same as sweet-smelling luxuries (103–4). Palinurus outright calls her a hound (112). The actor playing Leaena probably crawled around on all fours, sniffing and snorting and cavorting like a dog on the trail.

Figure 3.1 A nut weevil. "Nut Weevil," by Katrin Schulz, 2014, CC BY-SA 2.0.

The banker also has an animal name: Lyco suggests the Greek word *lukos*, "wolf." His name reflects the common portrayal of bankers in Roman comedy as greedy, grasping, cunning, untrustworthy, and opportunistic, just like the modern animalistic insult "loan shark." Lyco conforms to the stereotype. He argues, he cheats, he pushes Cappadox to break his oath.

Two smaller moments round out the animal theme in *Curculio*. First, when Phaedromus visits Planesium at play's open, she complains that Palinurus annoys her, and he doesn't take it well in his reply: "What're you talking about, you dumpster fire? *You*, with your owl-lookin' eyes, are gonna call *me* a pain in the ass? Drunken munchkin! Trash!" (189–92). Let's set aside for a moment the surprising intensity of Palinurus' vituperation. His insult about Planesium's eyes uses animal imagery. The mask representing Planesium may even have had stylized decoration suggestive of her "owl eyes," since *persolla* also means "little mask."

Finally, the soldier's signet ring invokes an animal. Lyco describes the soldier's seal for us when he's doing business with Curculio disguised as "Summanus": a guy with sword and a shield, cutting an elephant in half (424). Therapontigonus is a blowhard not just in person but in choice of logo, too. Elephants were for Romans the most fearsome instrument of war, closely associated with the formidable armies of that Carthaginian general Hannibal, Rome's arch-enemy. For Therapontigonus' signet ring to depict a soldier felling an elephant in one stroke speaks volumes about his sense of self-worth.

Commerce and law

Financial and legal affairs form an undercurrent in *Curculio*. Phaedromus' basic obstacle to having Planesium is financial, since he lacks the cash to buy her and isn't legally old enough to receive a loan, while the ultimate resolution—identifying her as freeborn and thus a survivor of unlawful trafficking—is legal. Lyco the banker is an obvious representative of the play's financial elements. Phaedromus ends up taking on a legal role as arbiter in the play's final scene, where he deceitfully agrees to be an impartial judge of the dispute between Therapontigonus and Cappadox over payment for Planesium. The financial entanglements between Cappadox, Lyco, and Therapontigonus are sealed by a legal technicality, Cappadox' oaths. And whenever either Lyco or Cappadox think they're in trouble, they try to take the matter to the praetor, Rome's chief judicial magistrate, evidently because they think they'll be able to talk their way out of trouble in court.

In addition to overarching thematic elements, law and economics crop up throughout the play. Palinurus repeatedly invokes law in the play's opening when he is warning Phaedromus to be careful who he sleeps with. First, he raises the specter of *stuprum*, illegal sexual misconduct, when asking Phaedromus whether his erotic adventure is "a crime unworthy of you or your breeding . . . entrapment of a chaste girl or someone who should be chaste" (23–6). Then, Palinurus alludes to a potential punishment for adulterers, castration, with a pun on the word *intestabilis* ("unable to make a will"/"without testicles," 30–2, a threat made more explicit in the final scene of Plautus' *Miles Gloriosus*). Palinurus' solution to avoid legal pitfalls? Commerce: going for a love object that is openly for sale (33–5).

When Planesium joins Phaedromus on stage for their initial nighttime encounter, she says the sex-trafficker will never keep her away from him, "not unless death transfers my lifeforce away from you" (174). Planesium uses an odd word, *abalienauerit*, a legal term that refers to formal transfer or sale of property. This choice of imagery reminds us that Planesium herself is legally property and is herself threatened with being "alienated" from her current residence (with Cappadox) to the soldier—but her words here defiantly assert her humanness, her agency in having affection for Phaedromus. After Planesium has spoken, Palinurus interjects with some more legal language, suggesting he'd like to bring formal charges against Phaedromus for making poor erotic life choices (175–6).

Much later, when Curculio (in disguise) is leading Planesium from Cappadox' house to Phaedromus', the dialogue is filled with legal terminology. Cappadox uses the phrase for formal denial of a charge in court (*it infitias*, 489) as a colloquial figure of speech. When transferring Planesium over to Curculio, Cappadox uses the Roman legal formula for doing so (*mancipio tibi dabo*, 494), which sets Curculio off on a jargon-filled rant about how sex-traffickers are oathbreakers and lawbreakers by profession (494–8, 515).

Therapontigonus brings with him a financial and legal mess, which is matched with financial and legal terminology. In conversation with the banker, he refers to Planesium as "my merchandise" (564). When Phaedromus confronts him about having tried to purchase a freeborn girl, they enter into a dispute over going to court and Roman legal procedure for summoning witnesses (620–3). Then, once they've discovered Planesium's true identity and set aside their antagonism, they seal the deal of the marriage engagement (674):

Phaedromus Soldier, do you promise this woman to me to be my wife?

Therapontigonus I do promise.

Though this interchange sounds redundant, it is equivalent to signing a contract in the modern world.

One effect of the law and commerce motif is that the erotic plot of *Curculio* (Chapter 2) is again marked as unromantic. From start to finish, Planesium exists as a commodity. Phaedromus and Therapontigonus window shop for her and haggle over her with Cappadox, who treats her not as a human being but as a prized possession. Once she is recognized as freeborn, Planesium remains a commodity, exchanged between Therapontigonus and Phaedromus as a symbol of their alliance and of resolution of the dispute between Therapontigonus and Curculio.

At the same time, legal and economic language and plot points help make the play seem more realistic. Struggling to secure a loan, worrying over expenses and debts, trying to secure justice in the face of dishonest conduct by disreputable characters: all that would have been familiar aspects of daily life for many in the audience. And this thematic material underscores the play's message about uncertainty, both economic and interpersonal. You don't know who you can trust, who will trust you with a loan, who is freeborn and who isn't, who you can pursue a relationship with and who you can't.

Sickness

Disease both literal and metaphorical, both physical and psychological, plagues the imagery of Plautus' *Curculio*. The most prominent example is Cappadox' illness, which has him looking green in the face and swollen in the belly when he first appears. Illness is a natural choice of motifs for a play set in Epidaurus, the most important medico-religious site in the ancient Greek world, headquarters for the worship of the medical god Aesculapius (Greek: Asklepios): see Figure 3.2.

Figure 3.2 Remains of the sanctuary of Asklepios in Epidauros, Greece. Photo by T. H. M. Gellar-Goad, 2019.

The automatic connection between Epidaurus and medicine may actually have motivated Plautus, or the author of the Greek original he was adapting, to set the play in that town—or even inspired the play to begin with. The shrine of Aesculapius takes a prominent place as the center building represented on stage (and may be a joke for viewers who know the town, if the huge medical complex is replaced by a single house sandwiched between two others). Cappadox' exits from and re-entry into the shrine for medical rituals help drive the play's action.

Cappadox' disease doesn't seem to be contagious, but his house doesn't make for healthy living, either. His enslaved doorkeeper Leaena suffers from alcoholism. Although the ancient Greeks and Romans didn't talk about alcoholism as a pathology in the same sense as medical professionals do today, they did understand the damaging effects of addiction, including addiction to alcohol.

As Phaedromus approaches Cappadox' house at play's start, Palinurus calls him insane (19) for greeting Cappadox' door, and jokingly suggests the door itself might be feverish (17). Shortly thereafter, Palinurus says Phaedromus would make Venus (goddess of love) sick to her stomach (74). When Planesium and Phaedromus have their clandestine meeting, Palinurus calls Phaedromus "completely insane in love" (177).

The funniest bit of sickness motif comes from Curculio. In his first entrance, after saying hello to Phaedromus but before telling him how the trip to procure a loan went, Curculio looks pale from exhaustion (311), complains of being in bad health (312), and specifically lists some unusual symptoms (317–19):

> I'm dying, I simply can't see straight, my teeth are full of mucus, my throat's got pinkeye from hunger, that's how I'm doing, arriving with my tummy tired because of my lackitudiness of food.

These are some wacky medical terms. Curculio hilariously conflates different ailments of different body parts into weird hybrid diseases. He does so with alliteration typical of Plautus' wild style (*lippiunt fauces fame, | ita cibi uaciuitate uenio lassis lactibus*). He even invents a word: *uaciuitas* exists only here in all of surviving Latin literature. Curculio's self-diagnosis matches the quackery you'll find from doctors elsewhere in ancient comedy, both "real" (as in Plautus' *Menaechmi*) and "fake" (as with the sidekick pretending to be a medic in Menander's *Aspis*). Everyone knows that the best remedy is to stuff a cold—and Curculio is hoping that whatever his maladies are, Phaedromus will prescribe him a feast as his cure.

The theme of illness in *Curculio* asks us to step back and reflect on our own lives and perceptions. Phaedromus' affection for Planesium might seem like a cheesy performance at first, but Palinurus' commentary recasts it as an acute bout of mental illness. His strange take on their relationship makes space to reevaluate it, to think about the dynamics of power and socioeconomic status that lurk beneath the surface of the couple's flirtations. Stern, traditionalist Roman moralists in the audience might think it is indeed madness for a marriageable citizen youth to be spending all his time fawning on an enslaved sex-laborer.

Leaena's addiction, meanwhile, underscores the hazards enslavement poses to your health. When we turn to the immediate source of these ills, Cappadox, we find him ill, too. As he enters, he complains, "I'm walking around with my spleen squeezing me like a girdle, I feel like I've got twin sons in my belly. I'm super-afraid I'll burst right in the middle, poor me!" (220–2); Palinurus says he has "a swollen belly and greenish eyes" (231); and he tells Palinurus, "my spleen's killing me, my kidneys hurt, my lungs are being torn apart, my liver's torturing me, my heart's roots are dying, all my guts hurt" (236–8). In Cappadox' case, counterintuitively, the disease—disgusting and exaggerated though it may be—reminds us that he isn't an otherworldly monster or perfectly villainous supervillain, but a human, with a human body not so different from the bodies he buys and sells.

What's funny in *Curculio*?

Curculio is hilarious, and much (though not all) of the humor continues to resonate today. Throughout the play's early scenes, Phaedromus repeatedly tries to shut Palinurus up, with little success. At one point, Phaedromus notices that Leaena is about to bring Planesium out, so he says to Palinurus, "Shh! Shut up, shut up!" (156). Palinurus replies, "Jeez, of course, I'm shutting up!" (same line). It's hard to be quiet while explaining how quiet you're being. When Palinurus complains about having to stay up late because of Phaedromus' love connection, Phaedromus tells him to shut up again, setting off this exchange (182–4):

Phaedromus Shut up!
Palinurus What, *I* should shut up? Why don't *you* go to sleep?
Phaedromus I *am* asleep, don't shout at me.
Palinurus Oh, come *on*, you're totally awake.
Phaedromus Well, *actually*, I'm asleep, in my own way: this is how I sleep.

Palinurus finds this sort of nonsense perplexing every time Phaedromus throws it at him. The fact that Palinurus doesn't have the perfect comeback here is an early sign that he won't turn out to be a *seruus callidus* trickster.

When Curculio first rushes on stage, he delivers this epic rant about all the people in town who annoy him when he's in a hurry. When Curculio meets up with Phaedromus, he pretends to be overcome by physical weakness, as we just saw in discussing the theme of sickness. Phaedromus asks him what's wrong. His reply: "Shadows are overtaking me, my knees are collapsing from lack of food" (309). This is precisely the type of ailment you'd expect a parasite to have—lack-of-food poisoning. Phaedromus' rejoinder is understated: "dammit, I'm sure it's from exhaustion" (310). The banality of Phaedromus' comment is charmingly absurd. Plautus subsequently pulls another laugh line out of the parasite stock type, by having Curculio describe how his belly has a special compartment to store the leftovers of his leftovers (386–8).

Curculio keeps the laughs coming after he's gone undercover as the soldier's lackey. His mention of the soldier's ridiculously long name elicits humorous acknowledgment from Lyco: "Blergh, I recognize that name, 'cause I filled up four whole wax tablets with that name when I wrote it out" (410–11). And Curculio's own fake name is a joke: he says he earned the name "because when I've fallen asleep drunk, I wet myself [*uestimenta ... summano*]" (415–16). "Summanus" is a plausible name for a person, but also sounds like *summano*, "I make wet." It also links to the character of Palinurus, whose name can interpreted to mean "piss into the wind" or "piss again." Ancient potty humor can be matched with modern: a 2019 production of *Curculio* by my Wake Forest University students replaced the name Summanus with "Lou Sanis" (switching urine for diarrhea).

Cappadox has a fair share of wit, too, which he brings to bear especially against the soldier. At their first greeting, Cappadox pretends he's about to invite Therapontigonus to dinner with the formal "today at my place ..." (562)—only to assure the soldier, "... you'll never even lick a single grain of salt" (same line). Cappadox' rude punchline provokes Therapontigonus to emulate it, with middling results: "Thanks for the invitation, but I've got plans ... for things to turn out bad for you" (563).

Cappadox later plays on Curculio's name meaning "weevil" (586–7). Just before this, Therapontigonus complains that Curculio stole his ring (*anulus*), which Cappadox intentionally misunderstands to mean "little anus" (*anulus*), letting him turn it into a homoerotic sex joke (584–5): "You lost your asshole? Neat, the soldier's been commissioned into a busted-ass battalion!" The switch from second person ("you've lost") to third ("the soldier's been") indicates that Cappadox has turned to the audience to crack this joke. He's doing stand-up comedy at Therapontigonus' expense.

Even when Cappadox suffers his comeuppance at play's end, he still brings the banter. After Phaedromus accuses Cappadox of breaking his oath, an oath made with his tongue, Cappadox says, "Well, now I say I didn't, with the same body part. It was born to me for speaking, not for losing cash" (705–6). The stock type of the sex-trafficker is always assumed to be an oathbreaker by default, and here Cappadox explains that tendency to perjure on pseudobiological grounds.

What about the original audience in ancient Rome? No evidence survives about what ancient audiences thought about *Curculio* specifically. We will probably never pick up a lot of funny things in the play. At the same time, a lot of the jokes hold up, and a lot of what we (or at least I) find funny in *Curculio* probably felt that way to its original audience.

Something we can't automatically understand the same way a Roman audience would is parody, and *Curculio* includes some excellent moments of parody, big and small. Phaedromus parodies a religious hymn or magic spell when he sings to the bolts on Cappadox' door in hopes that they'll open and let Planesium come out (149–55). Likewise Leaena, once she's taken her bribe of wine from Phaedromus, parodies ritual and prayer formulas in giving a begrudging "first-fruits" offering to Venus (125). The unnamed cook character also parodies religion when he gives Cappadox a sham dream-interpretation (259–73). Finally, after Planesium and Therapontigonus realize they're family and she is engaged to Phaedromus, Curculio hungrily talks about not only a standard *wedding* feast (*cena nuptialis*, 661) but also a *sibling* feast (*cena sororia*, 662), which is not actually a standard practice but something Curculio invents in hopes of an extra free meal. These jokes play on aspects of daily life that would be familiar to most members of the audience, even if they require explanation and contextualization for us.

Plautus also writes jokes the original audience might have found funny that I do not. Slapstick—by which I mean staged violence—figures prominently in Phaedromus' interactions with Palinurus in the play's opening scenes and in a brief fistfight between Curculio and Therapontigonus near its close (623–7). Phaedromus hits Palinurus whenever he talks back or says something rude about Planesium or doesn't keep quiet; in other words, Phaedromus abuses a man enslaved to him for not complying with his demands. Curculio, still disguised as Summanus, strikes Therapontigonus because the soldier suggests he's enslaved, not free. Therapontigonus reciprocates.

Free men in this play use violence to enforce status. This correlation of status and physical abuse connects to the systematic use of torture to enforce power structures in enslaving societies across history and across the world, including the enslaving societies of ancient Greece and Rome. Given the prominent role of enslaved characters in Plautus' comedies, it's no wonder that torture of enslaved persons crops up here and elsewhere. But it should make all modern viewers of Plautine theater pause, take a step back, and ponder the historical abuses of countless humans that are reflected in the jokes and gags.

A final element of what's funny about *Curculio* is something we can't derive from just reading the text. Theater is performative, and much of its payoff comes in performance. Plautus' plays feature lots of stage action, costuming, slapstick, visual gags, song, and dance. Chapters 4 and 5 explore how *Curculio* might have sounded and looked.

4

Curculio in Performance: Music, Song, and Dance

The only thing about *Curculio* that survives is the text, 729 lines of Latin. Nothing but dialogue, either: no stage directions, prop lists, song sheets, or choreography. Yet, the performance included music, singing, dancing, masks, costumes, scenery, and physical comedy. It would have been bright and brash and ridiculous and hilarious. In this chapter, we'll cover music; in Chapter 5, what the actors wore and what they did on stage.

Plautus' theater was musical theater. Over half of the lines he wrote were to be delivered by the actors with musical accompaniment; I agree with Timothy J. Moore's argument that all accompanied lines would be sung. In *Curculio*, about 55 percent is sung. Plautus composed the music as well as writing the words. His actors and **tibicen** (musician accompanist) might not know how to read, so they would have learned all the music and dialogue by ear from Plautus, or from the acting troupe's leader, if Plautus himself wasn't involved in rehearsing the play. The tibicen played the tibiae, a pair of pipes with double-reed mouthpieces: like an oboe but louder, reedier, and able to play two notes at once (Figure 4.1). The tibicen would play in unison with the singers, which means they would match up in melody and rhythm.

Rhythm is the fundamental building block of not only Plautus' comedy but also all Greek and Roman poetry, including theater. Every syllable of every word in Greek or Latin is either "long" or "short," and Graeco-Roman poetry consists of particular patterns of long and short syllables. A long syllable is approximately as long as two short syllables.

Plautus' metrical variety—and therefore his musical variety—is unsurpassed in Roman literature. He uses dozens of different metrical

Figure 4.1 In this section of a fresco in the "Tomb of the Diver" in Paestum, Italy, from approximately 470 BCE, a partier (*left*) plays the auloi, the Greek analogue to the Roman tibiae, for his erotic companion. Richard Mortel, 2019, CC BY 2.0.

forms, sometimes in longer passages of repeated meter (and thus repeated melody), sometimes in virtuosic **cantica** ("songs" or "show-stoppers"), where the meter changes as often as every line. Only one of the "countless meters" (*numeri innumeri*, as described in an ancient epitaph attributed to Plautus) is spoken rather than sung, the **iambic senarius**. He uses different meters to express different emotions, different kinds of characters, different paces of action. Imagine the complex leitmotif in Wagner's operas, or the character-specific melodies in film scores from *Star Wars* or *Lord of the Rings*. The rhythms of Plautus are on the whole more complex and less familiar than music in movies or on TV—and, probably, same goes for the tunes.

Plautus tends to structure his plays into "arcs" organized by changes in music. He doesn't use "acts" or "scenes"; those are modern terms, first applied to ancient theater in the Renaissance. The arc usually consists of rising action in spoken meter (iambic senarius), followed by falling action in sung meters. The sung parts are either extended passages of a single meter, or a mixed-meter **canticum**, or both. There is no set number of arcs and no fixed length for an arc. The rising and falling parts are not necessarily equal.

The musical structure of *Curculio* is unusual but not unparalleled for a Plautine play. (My analysis here assumes that the text of the play isn't missing major chunks of what Plautus wrote: see Chapter 9.) *Curculio* has four arcs, as shown in Table 4.1.

Table 4.1 The musical structure of Plautus' *Curculio*.

Arc	Action	Music type	Lines	What's happening
1	Rising	None (iambic senarii)	1–95	Phaedromus and Palinurus process to Cappadox' house
	Falling	Canticum	96–157	Leaena receives wine from Phaedromus, who sings to the door
		Repeated section (**trochaic septenarii**)	158–215	Planesium and Phaedromus' encounter
2	Rising	None (iambic senarii)	216–79	Cappadox seeks dream-interpretation from Palinurus and cook
	Falling	Repeated section	280–370	Curculio enters, fills Phaedromus in
3	Rising	None (iambic senarii)	371–461	Curculio persuades Lyco and Cappadox to give Planesium to him
	False start	Repeated section (trochaic septenarii)	462–86	Monologue of the Choragus
	Rising	Repeated section (iambic septenarii)	487–532	Curculio, Lyco, Cappadox transfer Planesium to Phaedromus' house
	Falling	Repeated section (trochaic septenarii)	533–634	Therapontigonus argues with Lyco and Cappadox; Planesium pursues Curculio to ask about the ring
4	Rising	None (iambic senarii)	635–78	Recognition, marriage arrangement
	Falling	Repeated section (trochaic septenarii)	679–729	Punishment of Cappadox

Four arcs is a common setup for Plautus, who has that many also in *Aulularia*, *Casina*, *Mercator*, *Mostellaria*, and *Pseudolus*. What is more unusual is that *Curculio* has only a single canticum, in arc 1. All of Plautus' plays have at least one canticum, and besides *Curculio* only *Asinaria* and *Miles Gloriosus* have just one. The third arc is the longest in the play. The final arc is the shortest, at just 95 lines.

Another noteworthy feature of *Curculio* is that almost all of the sung sections after the initial canticum use the exact same meter, trochaic septenarius. (The exception is a passage in arc 3 that uses the iambic septenarius, the meter of love and love objects, 487–532.) Trochaic septenarius is the single most common line type in Plautus, at 41 percent of Plautus' total lines, more even than the spoken iambic lines in Plautus' comedy. Here's a sample line of English trochaic septenarius that I just came up with:

— ⏑ —⏑— ⏑ —⏑ — ⏑ — — —⏑ —
Plautus uses complex meters. Don't despair: they're really cool!

In part because of its frequency, trochaic septenarius can convey a lot of different things to the listener. Chief among its effects are forward motion in plot or characters, false starts that emphasize important words, and the endings of plays.

In *Curculio* specifically, trochaic septenarii predominate—accounting for 41 percent of the play (297 out of 729 lines), same as Plautus' overall average. As a result, they serve as a central structuring element of the play, the architectural foundation of its music. Once the canticum in arc 1 is done, trochaic septenarii show the play is really getting started. When the music cuts out with the last bit of trochaic septenarii, we know we've moved on to the next arc; and when it cuts back in with another stretch of trochaic septenarii, we know we've reached the turning point of the current arc, and are headed towards the arc's end. This technique is not unique to *Curculio* among Plautine comedies, but the regularity of it is. *Curculio* has the simplest musical structure of any play by Plautus. This is not simply a byproduct of its length, since some of Plautus' most musically complex plays are on the shorter side, while some of his simplest (sometimes thought to be evidence that they were composed early in his career) are among his longest. In a play whose storyline divides into three mostly distinct subplots, with most characters involved really only in one or maybe two of them, the reliable sequence of meters helps bring a sense of unity and cohesion to the comedy as a whole.

Music and meter in the play's opening

Arc 1 opens with a spoken section as long as the entirety of arc 4. These first 95 lines include lots of plot exposition, good to set out clearly in unaccompanied speech: Phaedromus is after Planesium, but the sex-trafficker is demanding cash that Phaedromus doesn't have, so he's sent his parasite off to seek a source of funding overseas. Of speaking characters, only Phaedromus and Palinurus appear in this initial run of spoken verse. The canticum that follows (96–157), initiated by Leaena in her first appearance on stage, runs almost as long as the spoken "rise." It contains Leaena's entry monologue; some interchanges between the three about wine and Planesium; Leaena's exit to fetch Planesium; and Phaedromus' song to the bolts on Cappadox' front door. The trochaic septenarii of arc 1 (158–215) showcase the meeting of Planesium and Phaedromus, and the arc ends as everyone goes back into their own houses.

Interestingly, arc 1 both begins and ends with an empty stage. Leaena brings the music with her when she comes out of Cappadox' house and the music stops when the stage clears. Shortly before the canticum begins, Phaedromus draws our attention with his address of the door (88–9):

C'mon, my dear doors, drink, drink up, and willingly be propitious to me!

⏑ ⏑⏑ ⏑ ⏑ ⏑ — — — ⏑—
agite bibite festiuae fores;
⏑—⏑ —⏑ — ⏑— — ⏑ ⏑⏑—
potate, fite mi uolentes propitiae.

The long string of short syllables, the alliteration and other repetition of sounds, and the rhythmically emphatic ending all mark Phaedromus' words as important, as not-quite-everyday speech. It might also signal that a more metrically elaborate canticum is just around the corner. This canticum has never before been fully analyzed in English-language scholarship, so I'm going to provide a lot of detail.

The sole canticum of *Curculio*

Leaena enters, tracking down the scent of the wine Phaedromus has brought for her (96–100), using four different line types in her first five lines: diphilius, anapestic quaternarius, iambic dipodium with cretic colon, and iambic quarternarius. You don't need to worry about what the specific words indicate, and I won't list the meter of every single line. These give a taste of how rhythmically sophisticated and complex Plautus' songwriting is.

The canticum can be broken down into three parts: Leaena's solo (96–109, Part A); the long segment featuring her, Phaedromus, and Palinurus (110–46, Part B); and Phaedromus' song outside the door that separates him from Planesium (147–57, Part C). But I think that, when you look at the meter more closely, a finer-grained subdivision into 10 musical units makes more sense, as shown in Table 4.2.

From this schematization, we can make a number of observations about how Plautus has composed this canticum.

First, there isn't really a trio to speak of, since Leaena and Palinurus never have any back and forth. Phaedromus is their intermediary, or perhaps just the center of the scene's attention. Second, the choice of meter fits neatly with what's going on during the song. Palinurus and Phaedromus converse in anapests ⏑⏑—. The parody of religious music (Leaena's ode to wine, Phaedromus' hymn to the door, both to return to us in Chapter 7) employs cretics —⏑—, and Leaena's begrudging offering to Venus, an actual deity, comes in iambs ⏑—. Interactions between Leaena and Phaedromus are less regular and rhythmically more

Table 4.2 The musical structure of the *canticum* of Plautus' *Curculio*.

Unit	Lines	What's going on	Predominant meter(s)
1	96–100	Leaena hunts down and finds wine	None: mixed meters
2	101–9	Leaena's ode to wine	Mostly cretics —⌣—
3	110–13	Palinurus and Phaedromus banter	None: iambics ⌣— and Trochaics —⌣ create a hybrid cretic/anapestic feel
4	114–22	Leaena and Phaedromus talk	Bacchiacs ⌣—— and cretics
5	123–4	Palinurus and Phaedromus banter	Anapests ⌣⌣—
6	125–7	Leaena makes offering to Venus	Iambics
7	128–33	Palinurus and Phaedromus banter	Anapests
8	134–9	Leaena and Phaedromus talk; Leaena exits	None: mixed meters
9	140–6	Palinurus and Phaedromus banter	Anapests
10	147–57	Phaedromus' hymn to the door	Mostly cretics

jumbled—perhaps a subtle sign of the conflict between Phaedromus and the head of Leaena's household, Cappadox. Third, cretics and anapests dominate the canticum, and other meters that show up often have a cretic or anapestic feel to them (or elements of both cretics and anapests). In Plautus, in general, cretics can communicate surprise, jumpiness, bounce, and farce; anapests, meanwhile, can communicate exuberance, discoveries, panic, fury, joy, and seduction. In the canticum of *Curculio*, in particular, these associations are borne out. Mock-religious speech is farcical, as is Leaena, so both are good fits for cretics. Meanwhile, anapests are a good choice for Palinurus and Phaedromus, because one is furious at staying up late and losing wine to the sex-trafficker's doorkeeper, while the other is anxious and horny and desperate.

Let's dive into the units in a little more detail.

[1/Part A] The diphilii —⏑⏑—⏑⏑———⏑⏑—⏑⏑— we hear from Leaena as she enters (96–7) have a pretty regular, anapest-like feel to them: *boom-ba-dah boom-ba-dah boom boom boom-ba-dah boom-ba-dah boom.* Anapests are the classic meter for when a Greek chorus comes on stage, with a marching cadence and beat, and Plautus may pick up on that association here. Even if not, the sense of vigorous motion in the rhythm helps emphasize Leaena's hound-dog pursuit of the wine. These first two lines consist each of two identical units symmetrically flanking a single central long syllable:

The flower of old wine has been launched at my nostrils. Love for it draws me out here through the shadows. I want it bad.

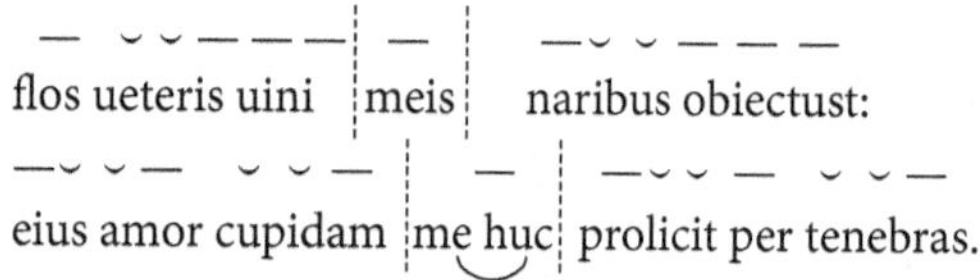

Her subsequent lines leading up to the ode to wine show similar symmetry, but it's not perfect like it is in these first two. After an anapestic entrance with two diphilii plus an actual line of anapests (98), two iambic lines allow Leaena to rhythmically shift gears towards cretics as she prepares to sing her ode.

[2] The ode to wine is mostly made up of cretics, which can bring a solemn atmosphere to the stage. This ode divides into two "stanzas" (forgive my anachronism): 101–4 and 105–9. The first stanza is punctuated with an ithyphallic coda —⏑—⏑—— ("I want to be buried [whenever you, wine, are poured out]," *peruelim sepultam,* 104). This ending is jokey—Leaena loves wine so much she's ready to die on the ground it's spilled on—and the same ithyphallic rhythm is used for two more wine punchlines later in the canticum, when Phaedromus tells Palinurus that Leaena's wine-drinking is limited to only a few gallons at a time (100), and when Leaena says it's been far too long since she's had a drink (121a). The second stanza of the ode to wine is remarkably regular, with twenty cretics in a row, only

one (the nineteenth) appearing as anything other than the usual —⏑— rhythm.

[3/Part B] In Palinurus and Phaedromus' first bit of chatter, iambic and trochaic lines are combined with a cretic line for a mixed cretic-anapestic feel, which blends together the two principal forms that have appeared in Leaena's solo. Line 112a furnishes the only instance of catalexis in the play. Catalexis refers to the cutting-off of the final syllable or beat that's "supposed" to occur in a line of poetry. It often conveys closure, and in this scene of *Curculio*, it marks the end of Palinurus and Phaedromus' eavesdropping. The very next line is Phaedromus saying, "I guess I have to get this old lady's attention" (113).

[4] When he does draw Leaena's attention, Phaedromus addresses her in bacchiacs (114, 117–18), which have a ⏑—— rhythm that comes off as mock-solemn. It is almost as if Phaedromus is experiencing a divine epiphany, as if Leaena is a goddess visiting him down here on earth. 116–117 stand out in particular, with lots of alliteration on S and a **tricolon** in the first line ("[the god of wine] is coming to soothe your thirst, since you're sputtering, so thirsty, semi-sleepy," *tibi … screanti, siccae, semisomnae* | … *sitim sedatum*). Leaena will soon echo Phaedromus' alliteration when Phaedromus greets her with a customary "hope you're well!": "how could I be doing well when I'm parched with thirst?" (*egon salua sim quae siti sicca sum?*, 120).

But Leaena quickly persuades Phaedromus to switch from bacchiacs to cretics, by using cretics of her own (115, 119–21). I think we might consider that cretics—and the now lost melodies that would have gone with them—are the motif of Cappadox' household. Leaena, and Phaedromus following her, use notably regular cretics, with few substitutions to the default —⏑— pattern. The side chatter between Palinurus and Phaedromus is, by contrast, more anapest-like: moving the plot along, rushed interjections and side conversations, anxiety and excitement and impatience. Or maybe cretics in *Curculio* are the rhythm of praise, since they appear in both Leaena's ode to wine and Phaedromus' hymn to Cappadox' door.

[5–6] Palinurus quickly tires of the conversation between Leaena and Phaedromus, so he tries to move the action along with anapests (123–4). He prompts Phaedromus to give Leaena the wine they've brought, which, in turn, prompts her offering to Venus (125–7):

> Venus, from my little bit, I'll give you an itty-bitty little bit, and I'm not happy about it. 'Cause lovers and drunkards, when they're trying to get on your good side, they give you wine, but I don't often get this kind of jackpot.

> ⏑ — — — — — ⏑ — — ⏑ ⏑ ⏑ — ⏑ — —
> Venus, de paulo paululum hoc tibi dabo haud lubenter.
> — ⏑ ⏑ ⏑ — — ⏑ ⏑ ⏑ — — — — — — — —
> nam tibi amantes propitiantes uinum dant potantes
> — — ⏑ — — — ⏑ — — — — — ⏑ — —
> omnis, mihi haud saepe euenunt tales hereditates.

Leaena sings in iambic septenarius, the meter of love in Roman comedy, a fitting choice for an offering to the goddess of love and sex, and a divergence from this scene's use of cretics for ritual-esque speeches. The second line comes with rhyming (*amantes*, *propitiantes*, *potantes*) and another tricolon (underlined). These features and especially the abundance of long syllables in Leaena's song generate a sense of solemnity, of ritual weight as she intones her offering to her goddess. On the third line, the enjambment of *omnis*—how it spills over from the end of the previous line—underscores the abundance of Venus' wine in contrast to Leaena's.

[7] Palinurus interrupts the mood with more banter in anapests (128–33), with lots of fast syllables. This is most prominent in the only direct interchange between Leaena and Palinurus in the whole canticum (131):

> **Leaena** Whoa!
> **Palinurus** 'Sup? You liking it?
> **Leaena** Totally liking it!
> **Palinurus** Well, *I'd* totally like to stab you with a cattle-prod.

LE. ah! PA. quid est? ecquid lubet? LE. lubet! PA. etiam mi quoque
stimulo fodere lubet te.

The word *lubet*, "like it," recurs a lot here, with three repetitions, and another to follow at 136.

[8] When Leaena exits into the house to bring out Planesium (139), she does so in anapests, again giving a rhythmic drive to her motion on stage. The exact rhythm of her line is perfect for grabbing attention and conveying the importance of her exit:

> Just make sure I don't go thirsty and I'll bring out what you're in love with.
>
> tu me curato ne sitiam, ego tibi quod amas huc adducam.

Palinurus and Phaedromus pick up on these anapests in their ensuing chitchat. Here, as before, Phaedromus seems to take his musical cues from Leaena.

[9] Right after Leaena's exit, Phaedromus promises to build a statue in her honor, "I'll set up not a golden statue but a wine-y one" (140a):

> uineam pro aurea ¦ statua statuam.

This line, cut down the middle, is a perfect mirror image, two dactyls —˘˘ followed by two anapests ˘˘—. The anapestic second half is a doublet of its own in terms of both rhythm and content. It is a rhetorical device known as *figura etymologica*, "etymological phrase," since *statua* refers to the statue and *statuam* to building the statue. When Phaedromus turns to Palinurus to talk about how lucky he'll be if he can see Planesium (141–41a), he stays in the same meter but uses more spondees —— instead of short anapests ˘˘—, emphasizing the weight of his emotion.

Lines 143–4 are similarly spondaic, slow, and deliberate—a good fit here, since Phaedromus is telling Palinurus and the audience a key plot point, that he's sent Curculio out for cash. Plot exposition within song is unusual. Typically, it is spoken clearly in the one non-sung meter of Roman comedy, like all the love-story explanation at the beginning of the play. It makes sense to slow down the music when we're hearing something important for the first time; and the music speeds back up right after the plot exposition is done (145–6). These lines also feature a rhythmic call and response between the two men:

> **Phaedromus** How about I go to the doors and sing at them?
> **Palinurus** If you want. I don't prohibit it or encourage it, master, since I've figured out that your character and nature have totally changed.

— ⌣⌣ — ⌣⌣ — — — — — ⌣ ⌣ — ⌣⌣ — ⌣ ⌣—

PH. quid si adeam ad fores atque occentem? PA. si lubet, nec ueto nec iubeo,

— ⌣⌣— ⌣⌣ — — — — — ⌣ ⌣ — ⌣ ⌣ — ⌣ ⌣—

quando ego te uideo inmutatis moribus esse, ere, atque ingenio.

Phaedromus' half of the first line gives a jaunty rhythmic model of two dactyls —⌣⌣ and two spondees — —, and Palinurus responds with a close parallel, replacing the first spondee with a dactyl and cutting the second half of the second dactyl. Then, in a whole line to himself, he uses the same exact rhythm as he and Phaedromus had in the previous line. This likely means the melody is the exact same for each line, too. Take note of all the **elisions** in this passage, marked with curved lines under the words: elision is where the final vowel in a word is cut out when the next word begins with a vowel, and in this dialogue, it shows how hurried and excited Phaedromus and Palinurus both are.

[10/Part C] Finally, the first eight lines of Phaedromus' hymn to the door (147–54) are unusually regular. Each line is the same (four cretics —⌣— apiece), with almost no variations (only a single instance of ⌣⌣ substituted for a — at 149 and 152). Each line divides neatly in two, with a break in the meaning or grammar of the words between the line's first two and last two cretics. Other interesting poetic features: the first two lines (147–8) repeat "door-bolts" twice and "you" in reference to those bolts four times. Line 149 has a lot of alliteration on *m* sounds (*gerite amanti mihi morem amoenissumi*, "be delightful and do what I desire!"). And in the second half of 153, when Phaedromus becomes irritated at the bolts because the door's not opening, he rhymingly calls them *pessuli pessumi* ("Worst. Bolts. Ever.").

Phaedromus' hymn to the door is important not only to the canticum and to *Curculio* but also to the history of Roman literature. It is the earliest surviving example in Latin of a paraclausithyron, "a song in front of a locked door." The paraclausithyron is a song type that originated in ancient Greek erotic drinking poetry: a young man—infatuated with a woman who's giving him the cold shoulder, not letting him in for sex—gets drunk, goes to her house, and sings (that part is the paraclausithyron itself). Plautus often writes paraclausithyron-like scenes, but no other songs as we have here in *Curculio*. The paraclausithyron scenario becomes an archetypal and recurring component of later Roman erotic poetry, especially in the works of Catullus, Propertius, and Ovid.

Phaedromus finishes his part of the song, and Plautus wraps up the whole canticum, with three lines consisting of more rare metrical forms, a wilamowitzianus and a cretic colon. This metrical arrangement unifies the song's overarching use of anapests and cretics. Doing so helps provide closure for the canticum, and allows for a rapid-fire threepeat of *tace*, "shut up!," in six short syllables in a row at 156. Another tool for closure is Cappadox' door, the very same one that Phaedromus has just been serenading. The first time it opens during the play, when Leaena comes out hunting for wine, is the start of the canticum and the play's music altogether. The next time it opens, when Leaena comes out again, this time with Planesium in tow, the canticum stops, physically book-ended by the door.

Music in the rest of the play

Arc 1 concludes with a longish section of trochaic septenarii (158–215), the go-to meter for sung sections in *Curculio*. Trochaic septenarii can always signal that plot action or character development is picking up speed, and trochaics here mark the big reveal, Planesium's entry on stage. The music in this section underscores the fact that we're watching a centerpiece of the comedy's storyline, the romance (or "romance") between her and Phaedromus.

Two more quick notes are in order on poetic effects in arc 1. First, the anapestic feel of the canticum occasionally returns, as when Planesium, exiting back into Cappadox' house, leaves Phaedromus with these words (213):

> If you really love me, buy me, quit asking about it, I'll make sure you get your money's worth.
>
> ⏑ ⏑ — ⏑ ⏑ — ⏑ ⏑ — ⏑ ⏑ — ⏑⏑— — — ⏑—
>
> si amas, eme, ne rogites, facito ut pretio peruincas tuo.

Planesium rushes inside to avoid being caught by the sex-trafficker as he returns from his visit to the shrine next door, and she does so with a fast-paced line that mimics the marching cadence of anapestic meter.

Second, a little earlier in the scene, Phaedromus expresses his joy at seeing Planesium with a poetic priamel, a common technique in lyric poetry, consisting of a list of alternatives that lead up to the item of real focus (178–80):

> Let kings keep their kingdoms to themselves. Let the wealthy have their wealth, their elected office, their courage, their fights, their battles. As long as they don't hate on me, let every person keep for themselves what's theirs.

Phaedromus is making an allusion to the sixth-century Greek lyric poet Sappho—or, at least, Plautus is. One of the most famous surviving fragments of her poetry opens with the statement, "some say an army of horses is the best thing upon the black earth, some an army of infantry, and some a fleet of ships. But I say it's whatever someone loves" (16.1–3). This allusion, to probably the most famous erotic poet in Plautus' (and Phaedromus') own time, hammers home the love story of this portion of the play, elevates Phaedromus' dalliance with an enslaved sex-laborer to the eternal beauty of Sapphic verse, and reminds the audience how far Phaedromus veers away from the norms of Roman (toxic) masculinity, with its high valuation of warfare, politics, and aristocratic wealth generated from enslaved labor in agricultural concentration camps. It also imports a lyric sentimentality to the music of the nighttime tryst between Planesium and Phaedromus.

Arc 2 begins with the first appearance of Cappadox (216). He comes on stage with spoken iambic senarii, as the music stops. This often happens with blocking characters like the sex-trafficker, because the audience is more likely to side with somebody who's singing. Cappadox' whole scene lacks music (216–79). It is Curculio himself who brings back the music, performing his grand entrance in trochaic septenarii (starting at 280). I find cosmic justice in the music of arc 2: Cappadox, the major obstacle, has no music, whereas Curculio, the character at the center of the plot, restarts the action at high speed when he arrives in town, singing up a storm.

Music leaves the stage along with Curculio (370) as we enter the play's long third arc (371–634). Once again, the music stops for the entrance of a blocking character undeserving of the audience's empathy: Lyco the banker. Like Cappadox, Lyco is involved in a trade that the Roman citizen elites found distasteful. To make matters worse, he is, like Cappadox, involved in the oppressive economics of sex labor and enslavement that are keeping Planesium unfree. And like Cappadox, he receives no musical accompaniment. Fittingly, Cappadox joins in on this music-less scene towards its end (455–61).

The next music to arrive continues the play's pattern, as the Choragus (Chapter 7) performs trochaic septenarii. His entry might seem like it's a standard usage of this meter to keep things moving, but it's actually a false start. The short length of the passage, only 25 lines (462–86), is at heart a bunch of funny business, a kind of intermission from the plot. In the longer scene that follows (487–532), the sense of a false start is confirmed, because the music doesn't cut out but switches into a meter that *Curculio* only uses elsewhere in the canticum of arc 1 for Leaena's short offering to Venus (125–7): iambic septenarii, the meter of love and love objects. This scene shows the successful conclusion of Curculio's plot to extract Planesium from Cappadox' house and into that of Phaedromus next door. Curculio himself brings the change of meter, just as he brought music at the opening of arc 2. This scene in arc 3 has both Cappadox and Lyco sing. Since Curculio has tricked them, they are no longer blocking characters, so they give in to the music rather than stop it. The fact that they sing iambic septenarii in particular demonstrates that they have been conquered by the play's erotic subplot.

Once Planesium is safely inside Phaedromus' house, we finally begin our falling-action passage of trochaic septenarii (583–634) that will fill out the rest of arc 3. At 102 lines, it's the longest stretch of one meter type in the entire play, spoken or sung, and more than half again as long as the canticum. The music is introduced this time by the arrival of the soldier Therapontigonus. This may signal to the audience that, despite appearances and the expectations of the genre, he's not going to be much of a blocking figure. This is Therapontigonus' time in the limelight: he careens from an argument with the banker to an argument with the sex-trafficker to an argument with Curculio to an argument with Planesium. If trochaic septenarius is the meter of action and resolution, Therapontigonus is using it to the fullest.

Arc 3 stands out not only for its length but also for its structure. Arcs 1 and 2 begin and end with an empty stage: all characters have gone off somewhere or not yet entered. (Since Plautus didn't have a stage curtain he could bring down and pull back up to mark off units of action, an empty stage is one way to send a signal to the audience about the play's structure; in *Curculio*, the stage is empty before lines 1, 216, 274, 371, 462, 487, 533, and 590.) The transitions within those arcs between spoken and sung, between canticum and trochaic septenarius, take place while characters remain on stage. In arc 3, by contrast, every internal transition—from spoken to sung trochaic septenarius, from trochaic septenarius to iambic septenarius and back to trochaic—happens with an empty stage, largely facilitated by the once-in-a-lifetime appearance of the Choragus. Even more remarkable is that arc

3 doesn't end with an empty stage, but the transition to unaccompanied speech occurs in the middle of a scene. As Planesium entreats Therapontigonus, with increasing urgency, to tell her how he came by his ring, Therapontigonus transitions into spoken verse—stopping the music—to tell the tale (635). The switch mid-scene is an unexpected, powerful sign to the audience that serious business is afoot, and that we're about to hear an important backstory.

By the time we reach the end of arc 4's spoken section (678), the matter has been resolved: Planesium and Therapontigonus are reunited, Phaedromus and Planesium engaged, Curculio anticipating lots of free food in reward for his tricky work. As if taking a cue from the transition between arcs 3 and 4, the musical transition within arc 4 takes place on a full stage. Cappadox enters as the music begins (679), signaling the play's grand finale. Here the trochaic verse is doing its job as meter of closure. Cappadox' introduction of it signifies not only that he is an obstacle no longer, but also that he's doomed to the usual comeuppance sex-traffickers suffer at the ends of several plays by Plautus.

Dance

In closing, let's take a moment to think about the visual partner of music, dance. Unfortunately, this piece of the puzzle must remain mostly a question mark. The evidence for Roman practices of dance and gesture—both visual evidence from artistic representations and textual evidence from treatises about performance—is much later than the time of Plautus. Plautus' scripts rarely mention dance or indicate clearly how exactly the actors are embodying their movements. And yet, dance and gesture are two of the most powerful items in the theatrical toolbox, and I believe it was a big part of Plautine comedy in performance.

Dance in Roman comedy seems to have been generally a solo affair, and included many mimetic gestures (acting out specific actions). A good example is Curculio's entry monologue, where he plays the enslaved errand-runner, rushing on stage in song, possibly pushing through the audience on his way. He calls out lots of people he has no time for while he's on his mission, from magistrates (285–6) to sleazebags hanging out downtown (296–8). He probably has specific dance moves as he mentions each of them—imitating or mocking them in a stylized way. The last group in particular, "those slaves of scoundrels who play back and forth" (295), might itself refer to a kind of dancing. Or the "playing" might be homoerotic: men taking turns being top and bottom. Either way, the line practically begs for Curculio to mime some dance action as he sings it.

Similarly, when Phaedromus sings to the doors of Cappadox' house earlier in the play, he specifically mentions dance. He asks the door-bolts to turn into "non-Greek dancers" (150). The word I've translated as "non-Greek," *barbarus*, comes into English as "barbarian" and literally means "speaking-a-language-that-sounds-to-Greeks-like-barbarbarbarbar." In Plautus, it's often an inside-joke way of saying "Roman," as opposed to Greek. Native Italian traditions of dance seem to have involved a fair amount of jumping and leaping, which is what the bolts would need to do to unlock the door for Phaedromus. The term *ludius* can mean dancer or actor, so we have here a metatheatrical reference, as well. At the same time as Phaedromus of the Greek city Epidaurus asks the bolts to jump like a Roman (or other non-Greek) dancer, he is also asking them to become Roman actors, just like the person speaking from behind Phaedromus' mask.

5

Curculio in Performance: Stagecraft

Recreating the performance of an ancient drama from the bare remains of its text is a particular kind of detective work. It starts with several hundred lines of poetry in Latin (or Ancient Greek) and has to end in a multimedia extravaganza of song, dance, brightly painted masks, costumes, set, and energetic stage action. Luckily for us, Plautus was one of the world's great wordsmiths, and the words he smiths are key to unlocking what his plays were like in performance.

The rhythms of his language tell us about his music and, from there, about his choreography. His choice of stock characters determines masks and costumes, while the things those characters say help flesh out the particulars of mask decoration and costume accessories. Plot and characters both necessitate certain props, while others are directly mentioned in dialogue or are implied by how characters interact. Entrances, exits, and the speeches and conversations of characters in the play communicate staging, blocking, and action.

Masks

All ancient Greek and Roman scripted drama was masked. Actors wore full-face masks, sort of like the ones in Figure 5.1 (ignore the costumes, though).

They likely were a little bit larger than normal-sized human heads, which would help people watching from far off or with bad eyesight. Amy R. Cohen has shown it's possible they were made in a special way that wouldn't muffle your voice but would instead make it clearer and make it carry better, sort of like how the wooden sounding box of a violin or guitar increases the audibility of its strings.

Figure 5.1 Masks at a performance of a scene from Plautus' *Poenulus* by members of Compagnia Fondamenta Teatro e Teatri, in Sarsina, Plautus' hometown. Photo by T. H. M. Gellar-Goad, 2019.

The most prominent thing about masks, though, would be how they were decorated. Paint, fake hair, and other visual elements of a mask would quickly allow any viewer to identify the gender, age (young or old), and status (free or enslaved) of the character it portrayed. For gender, the key component is skin color: red for men, white for women. (Yes, the Greeks and Romans adhered to the gender binary and the essentialism of sex and gender.) These colors are not realistic ones. The Greeks and Romans were not white. Rather, the colors represent elites' sexist ideology that men should have skin darkened from being outside in the fields, the Forum, or the battlefield, while women should be pale from staying home, spinning wool, and making babies—plus maybe some pale-ifying makeup made out of powdered white lead.

Age would be easiest to tell from a mask's hair. Hair could be represented in a variety of styles and colors, but white hair is a clear signal of age. Greeks and Romans tended to have curly, unreflective black hair, so deviations from that norm, such as reddish hair (a feature associated with enslaved Thracians, for example), could identify a character as not born locally, and thus as either a non-citizen immigrant or an enslaved person.

The masks would be shaped and decorated in a wide variety of ways so that they could be distinguished from each other. With recurring stock characters like parasite or sex-laborer, masks in Roman comedy would also have been stereotyped. After seeing a couple plays, someone would know a character's type and maybe their personality well before learning their name. The reliability of stock masks allows for fun gags based on cheating audience expectations. In Plautus' *Persa*, for example, an enslaved character starts the play by whining about sex and cash like a citizen lover boy. In our own play, Curculio's first entrance has him acting not like the parasite's mask he wears but like an errand-boy *seruus currens*.

Masks are remarkable objects. Really skilled mask-actors, like the now unknown originals who performed Plautus' *Curculio*, can take a mask's static depiction of a face and make it come alive. Through body language, posture, gesture, movement, and head position and angle, the same mask can communicate a whole range of emotions, from basic to nuanced. Theater-goers swear that they see a mask change expression. Ancient masks' exaggerated physical features would help with this lifelikeness. Masks of clever characters might even have asymmetrical features, so that a turn of the actor's head would change the mask's entire look and mood.

Another crucial feature of ancient masks is their giant mouth-holes. Other than aiding sound transmission, mouth-holes can also direct audience attention. If one character is speaking, mouth-hole pointed at the audience, other characters on stage would naturally look at the speaker, pointing their mouth-holes in that direction. In effect, masks can act as spotlights, no electricity required. If one character is eavesdropping or sneaking up on another, the actor can show his character has no idea what's happening by never pointing his spotlight, his mouth-hole, towards the sneaky character. Or she can suddenly "snap" her mask towards the eavesdropper, showing they've been caught red-handed.

No actual masks used in ancient Graeco-Roman theatrical productions survive; so, what am I basing all this on? First, ancient art. Stone and ceramic representations of theater masks survive from all over the territories of ancient Greece and Rome, and they give a great sense of facial expressions and hairstyles. Mosaics and wall-paintings of scenes from Greek drama were popular and have survived in a number of different archaeological sites, especially Samos, where a whole house is essentially a fan shrine to the comic playwright Menander. Mentions of masks appear occasionally in ancient literature, including a couple times in Plautus, and discussions about masks survive in the Greek authors Theophrastus and Pollux.

Modern scholarship has pushed the possibilities of masks ever forward. Classics professors who have staged performances of ancient drama with masks, such as C. W. Marshall, have contributed experiential knowledge about how masks work and what they can do. Comparative studies of ancient theater alongside theories, techniques, and practices of modern acting have helped us fill in gaps in the historical record with educated guesses about how ancient actors would have used their masks. And experimental scholarship—attempts to reconstruct ancient masks with different materials and methods consistent with ancient visual evidence as well as the limitations and opportunities of ancient technology—offer a way for experiential and comparative work to fit plausibly into the original performance contexts.

Costumes

What about the rest of the actors' bodies? Like masks, clothes serve as markers of gender and status. Enslaved characters were dressed differently from citizens, although enslaved and free members of the same household may have dressed similarly (so someone enslaved by a soldier might have martial accoutrements, and so on). The basic costuming was as follows. Everyone wore a one-piece coverall, a *tunica* (Latin) or *chiton* (Greek). Women would additionally wear a *palla*, an overgarment often translated into English as "mantle," a word I think I've only ever seen actually used in English when it's translating the Latin word *palla*. Men would wear a cloak called *pallium* (Latin) or *himation* (Greek). Young men, and especially soldiers, would wear a *chlamys*, a shorter-length coat good for traveling. Travelers would wear a distinctive broad-brimmed hat called a *petasus*. In our play, Therapontigonus the soldier definitely wears a *chlamys* (632) and maybe a *petasus*, too; Curculio also may wear a *petasus*, as he makes his entry, returning to Epidaurus.

Costuming could also provide clues to character types. Think alluring clothes for a free non-citizen sex-laborer, *chlamys* for a soldier, and the like. It seems to be the case in Rome itself that acting troupes would rent or borrow costumes from the aedile in charge of the festival or from a choragus (see the end of the next section). Otherwise, costumes might have been owned by the troupe, to be reused as much as possible, and tweaked as needed.

Masks and costumes in *Curculio*

No evidence survives about masks and costumes in *Curculio* beyond the text itself. So, the following is based on my educated guesswork and that of Plautus scholars before me. Masks and costuming in *Curculio* could support the play's key themes. The animal theme, in particular, opens up lots of creative mask ideas. Curculio, the weevil, could have a long nose like the proboscis of his namesake, and jaws ready to gnash like mandibles. Lyco, the wolf, could boast lupine features, perhaps with prominent canines in the mask's mouth. Leaena, the wildcat, should have a leonine mask—and, maybe, given her advanced age, some whiskers. Planesium might have an animalistic mask, too, given what Palinurus says to her about her "owl eyes" (191; Chapter 3) when she insults him.

The theme of sickness actual and metaphorical can show up in masks and costuming both. Cappadox is the obvious one: he complains about a swollen liver and other characters remark on the discoloration of his skin, so his mask would be painted an unnatural color and his clothes would be comically overstuffed. If, as I suspect (see Chapter 8), the sex-trafficker is feeling better after his second stay in the shrine of Aesculapius, his re-entry on stage could feature a fresh mask (one that looks exactly like the earlier one but with the reddish skin typical for the mask of a healthy man) and normal clothing—or the actor could just move in a manner that expresses less pain and discomfort.

Phaedromus' lovesickness, too, can be represented visually. Maybe his symptoms include paleness, suggesting a mask paler than the usual man's red. Such an artistic decision would make Phaedromus stand out among other men, almost but not quite crossing the boundary line between the two genders. It would suggest he's spent too much time indoors—either at home pining over Planesium or in the sex-trafficker's den of sensual pleasure—and has endangered his manliness because of his erotic obsessions.

The title character, meanwhile, has his fair share of the costuming limelight. His rowdy running first entrance features a disparaging comment about "these damn Greeks with their damn cloaks" (288). This line is funny because it features a low-status (non-citizen?) actor in Rome playing a character who is literally a Greek in a *pallium*, a *Graecus palliatus*, complaining about *Graeci palliati*. His mention of their clothing is metatheatrical (Chapter 6), since the subgenre of comedy that *Curculio* belongs to is named *comoedia palliata* after that exact type of cloak. Curculio is half in character, half in real life—and he has no time or patience for any of it. He's too important to Phaedromus, to the play's plot, and definitely to himself to deal with a run-of-the-mill *comoedia palliata* scene or scenario. Curculio gives a wink and a nod to the audience here, revealing a little self-awareness that he's just a character in a fictional world, and acknowledging the important role of costuming in shaping that world.

This moment is hilariously meta—and also racist, as can be seen from Denise McCoskey's work on Roman anti-Greek invective more generally.

Curculio, who is supposed to be a Greek himself living in a Greek city, whines about the Greeks clogging up his city streets, in a way that sounds very Roman, with a flavor of distaste for immigrants that might remind you of a xenophobic relative or acquaintance. He is, after all, a character in a Roman comedy being performed in Rome, where Greeks were plentiful but often subjected to suspicion and outsider status.

Curculio takes advantage of his knowledge about costuming in a big way later on, when he disguises himself as "Summanus" right before he meets up with Lyco the banker (391). He puts on his disguise in a hurry—literally in the middle of a line—and immediately becomes unrecognizable as himself. Since Lyco greets him with "hey, one-eye!" (392), we know the disguise consists of an eyepatch. (Let's pause briefly here to note again an unpleasant pathway of Roman humor, making fun of non-normatively bodied people.) Once more, I think Curculio is acting outside the comedy as well as within it: he knows that putting on a distinctive and unusual costume element will automatically qualify him as a different character, even if all the rest of his gear is the same. This is how doppelgangers are kept separate in another of Plautus' plays, *Amphitruo*. And Curculio signals his costume-awareness by using a key word for acting, "I'll pretend" (391 again). Curculio here is again being metatheatrical.

Costume accessories take center stage at one point in the play, when Therapontigonus the soldier faces off against Cappadox the sex-trafficker. They're fighting because Therapontigonus is shocked that Cappadox has already handed Planesium off to somebody else, and Cappadox is certain he gave her over to Therapontigonus' authorized agent (574–80):

> **Therapontigonus** So help me, by my sword and shield [and . . .?] that help me in battle—if I don't get the girl back, I'll turn you into something the ants can carry away in little bits.
>
> **Cappadox** Well, so help *me*—by my tweezers, comb, mirror, curling-iron, clippers, and wipe-down cloth, I don't care about your fancy words and your big damn threats any more than the slave woman who cleans my toilet.

Therapontigonus makes his oath via a list of the standard props of a soldier character (though something's lost from 574, probably further recitation of his military gear).

Many read Cappadox' reply as an inversion of the soldier's kit—cosmetic rather than martial, domestic rather than external to home and city, and, most importantly from a patriarchal Roman perspective, effeminate rather than hypermasculine. That assumes Cappadox has those things for his own personal use. To me, it makes more sense to think of them as tools of his trade, as the essential gear of a sex-trafficker. In that case, he won't be using them on himself, but on his wares, the humans he enslaves as sex-laborers, to enhance their physical allure and therefore his profits. From this perspective, Cappadox is going toe to toe with Therapontigonus, matching his gear with the soldier's.

Something masks and costumes together would make clear is just how many different stock types are in *Curculio*. The ten different masks, each distinct from the next, would bring Epidaurus to life on the stage, giving it a feel of an actual town really populated by all types of people. Most would be wearing clothes typical of their gender and status. But Therapontigonus would be in military get-up, the more exaggerated and outrageous, the better. Cappadox would probably have more "exotic" costuming to represent his immigrant background—for a Roman audience, this might mean a pointy Phrygian cap, since that's an identifiable, stereotyped piece of garb associated with Asia Minor (modern-day Turkey/Anatolia, where both Phrygia and Cappadox' namesake land of Cappadocia were located).

A reason to think that *Curculio* is a comedy where the actors go all out for their costuming is the appearance of the Choragus (Chapter 7). He is literally supposed to be the guy that the theater troupe is renting or borrowing their costumes from. And he comes on saying he's worried Curculio won't return them (464). The Choragus is the bridge between the audience's world and the fictional world of Plautus' comedy—or maybe I should say he's the enchanted wardrobe that is a gateway not to Narnia but to Plautinopolis. If we haven't already been paying close attention to the actors' wardrobe up to now, we sure will be for the rest of the play.

Props

Theatrical props—stage properties—can perform a variety of functions, with three key categories identified by Robert Ketterer. First is **labeling**. A prop can tell us who a character is. Someone walking with a cane is an old person, and someone carrying a sword is a soldier. In *Curculio*, Therapontigonus the soldier would definitely have a sword, and Lyco the banker might have a prominent bag of cash or some scales to weigh payments.

The second category is the **mechanical function of props**. These items drive the plot forward. The sleeping potion in *Romeo and Juliet* fulfills this function, since it both foreshadows and facilitates the tragic demise of the title characters. The most important prop with a mechanical function in *Curculio* is Therapontigonus' ring, which has a pivotal role in Curculio's deception scheme, since it enables him to forge documents to extricate Planesium from Cappadox' household, and is the crucial token for the recognition scene. When Planesium sees it and learns that it's the soldier's, she realizes that he's her long-lost brother.

The third major function that props can take on in drama is **symbolic**. Such props communicate on a deeper level something about the characterization of the people in the play, or the play's mood, or the significance of the play's plot and themes. For example, during the procession at the beginning of *Curculio*, Phaedromus carries a candle. (Side note: the fact that he's carrying a light source tells the audience that it's nighttime, an instance of labeling.) Palinurus makes fun of him for carrying his own light: "you're your own slave boy, you're all dressed up and yet you're shining your own candle" (9). These lines suggest that the sight of a citizen man carrying his own lighting would seem incongruous. So, Phaedromus' prop symbolizes how out of sorts he is because of his infatuation with Planesium. Erotic desire has made him forget his status—or maybe we should even take the candle to characterize him as enslaved to love.

Stage properties in *Curculio*

Let's do a comprehensive analysis of props in *Curculio*. To begin with, here's an essential prop list:

candle (9)
ritual offerings for Venus ("breakfast"), maybe barley-cake (72)
wine jug (75)
water jug (160)
chair (311)
another water jug (312)
Therapontigonus' ring (first mentioned at 346)
tablets sealed with wax bearing the symbol on Therapontigonus' ring (347, 369, 412, 549, 551)
moneybag, supposedly containing 30 minae (a huge amount)
sword (567, 574, 632)
Planesium's ring (first mentioned at 653)

This list omits costume elements, some of which are important (for example, Curculio's eyepatch disguise), as well as props that aren't explicitly mentioned by the text but are probable or possible for a comic presentation of the play. A lot of the props are connected to each other in some way, especially through a series of exchanges.

We've already covered the candle that Phaedromus carries in the play's first scene, with its labeling and symbolic functions. It could also help with "spotlighting," drawing attention to whatever is the focal point on stage at any given moment, and it's a gift a poor Roman citizen client would give his wealthy Roman citizen patron, so it doubly underscores Phaedromus' surrender of status. Palinurus carries the wine jug, and someone from the procession (2) of enslaved attendants who follow Phaedromus probably carries the offerings to Venus, goddess of love and sex.

The wine jug is a double of the offerings, because Phaedromus initially sprinkles some of the wine onto Cappadox' door as if making a ritual **libation** (88–9), and because Phaedromus gives the jug to Leaena as a propitiatory offering, a gift to make her favorably inclined toward him as if she's a benevolent deity (122). While Phaedromus is offering a libation to the door, Palinurus mocks him by offering the door olives, meat, and capers (90); it could be funny if Palinurus had some snacks on hand that he just randomly pulled out. The gift of wine also initiates the first exchange of the play: wine in exchange for Planesium, albeit on a temporary basis. (Planesium, it turns out, is involved in a lot of these exchanges as an object, a troubling truth about the treatment of trafficked persons.) It also marks Leaena's shift from doorkeeper loyal to Cappadox to ally of Phaedromus. Leaena goes on to offer some of the wine to Venus in an actual libation (125–7), thus confirming the connection between the wine jug and the earlier "breakfast" for Venus.

Leaena returns to the stage with a jug of her own (160), with water to keep the door from creaking when she brings Planesium out—never mind that she's already opened and closed it twice for her own two entrances. The water, which she applies like medicine (161), can be seen as yet another libation. Taken together, the candle and the two vessels function as parodic versions of actual items that would be used in a religious ritual, a torch and a *patera* (a special kind of vase).

The next major props pop up in Curculio's first scene, where they are brought to help him recover from his running entrance. The chair marks Curculio as the center of the scene. Everyone else flutters around him like clients around a patron, a callback to Phaedromus as client with a candle in the play's early lines (another example of "Saturnalian inversion," Chapter 1). The water jug, meanwhile, connects this scene with Leaena. It's even possible that the same actor would have played both Leaena and Curculio, and if so, it could be funny for the actor as Curculio to be brought water from the same container that he, as Leaena, had previously brought on stage.

The real star of the props list is revealed for the first time at the end of this scene: the ring Curculio stole from the soldier (360). Since the design on the ring is so central to the recognition scene at the end of the play, Curculio probably has an oversized, even giant version of it to show off. That will help communicate to the audience how important the ring will be to what happens later. After all, the ring is the thing that ties together the three subplots of *Curculio*: it's stolen while Curculio is on an errand in support of Phaedromus' erotic entanglement, it's the tool that makes Curculio's deception feasible, and it's the recognition token that reunites Planesium and Therapontigonus.

The wax on the tablets Curculio forges calls back to the wax of the candle Phaedromus carried in his first appearance. Curculio tells Phaedromus he will have to write the forgeries based on Curculio's instructions. On the one hand, this probably means that Curculio himself is illiterate, a common experience for non-elites in ancient Rome. On the other hand, it puts Phaedromus into the (Saturnalian inversion-style) position of Curculio's *amanuensis* ("by-hand person"), an enslaved scribe who would write out what an elite Roman dictated, since elites tended not to do much of their formal writing in their own hand.

Therapontigonus' sword not only *labels* him as a soldier but also *symbolizes* his theatrical impotence. He brandishes and boasts about it again and again (567, 574, 632), and it features prominently in the design on his ring ("a man with a shield is cutting an elephant in half with his sword," 424). But, ultimately, despite being the only character with a weapon, he can't force anybody to do what he wants. Lyco brushes him off. Cappadox matches his sword with cosmetics equipment. Phaedromus legally outmaneuvers him, then takes over control of the scene to make sure Therapontigonus gets his money back from the sex-trafficker.

The money itself closes out the play. We see an onstage transfer, from Cappadox to Therapontigonus, in the second-to-last line of *Curculio* (727). Earlier, in an argument with Curculio, the soldier has explicitly equated the money with Planesium: "give me back the cash or the girl" (612). Therapontigonus turns out to be unsentimental about Planesium, until he discovers she's his sister: he's fine, so long as he receives a refund. His cold, calculating approach to Curculio lays bare the dehumanizing series of exchanges in which he is willingly—and Planesium unwillingly—involved.

The money, the tablets, and the soldier's ring are the most structurally significant props in *Curculio* as a whole. In fact, they represent the play's three subplots in reverse. The ring shows up first, and represents the recognition plot at the end of the play. The tablets are the physical instantiation of the play's second storyline, the deception. And the money, as we have seen, is equivalent to Planesium as sex object, the motivation for the erotic subplot at the beginning of the play. Each prop also connects thematically to its paired subplot. The ring was stolen by Curculio, just like Planesium was kidnapped from her family long ago. The tablets are forged, just like Curculio is disguised—a fake for a fake. The money issues from Cappadox' house into the possession of the citizen men, just as Planesium does. Finally, Planesium's and Therapontigonus' rings are like theatrical magnets, pulling the two of them together for their inevitable recognition and reunion.

The centrality of the ring in *Curculio* can be seen in its connections to other props. Every key prop in the rest of the play links back to the ring. The tablets are sealed with an impression of the ring's design. The design on the ring is what guarantees Lyco's delivery of the moneybag. The soldier's sword is itself depicted on the ring. And Planesium's ring is its duplicate. Therapontigonus' ring also serves as the mechanism for the play's most important exchanges. The ring allows Curculio to forge the tablets, which are how Lyco knows to give the money to Cappadox, who hands Planesium over to Curculio.

One last note on the ring of Therapontigonus. Curculio shows it off in his first scene, but afterwards he must take it off. Otherwise, he couldn't trick Lyco and Cappadox into thinking he's the soldier's agent, since said agent is supposed to have tablets sealed by the ring, not the ring itself. To that end, the tablets likely have a visible, oversized impression of the soldier's ring on them. It isn't strictly necessary for the play to work, but the visuals will be a useful (and, given the absurdity of the seal, comic) way to underscore the description in the dialogue. Curculio will subsequently put the ring back on while he is off stage, allowing for Planesium to see it (595). The size of the ring will provide visual reinforcement of Curculio's jokey dismissal of Planesium when she asks him about it: "what, like I've got your mom and dad hidden away under the gemstone?" (606). The ring is also a three-in-one package of prop functions. When we first see it on Curculio, it's mechanical, making the deception plot possible. When we learn it belongs to Therapontigonus, the ridiculous image labels him as a blowhard soldier. At play's end, the ring is not only mechanical—facilitating the recognition between Planesium and Therapontigonus—but also symbolic of new family bonds between former rivals Phaedromus and Therapontigonus.

Planesium possesses a copy of Therapontigonus' ring, but I don't think she wears it when we first see her. She definitely doesn't wear it *all* the time in her life generally—otherwise, presumably, Therapontigonus would have seen it when he was picking her out for purchase to begin with—and often the recognition tokens of a *uirgo intacta* like Planesium are hidden away in a chest or casket. In the play itself, she definitely has it on her at 653, but the fact that it's not been mentioned before then suggests she didn't have it in the earlier scenes. After all, since it would have to be big enough for the image to be legible to the audience, her wearing it would distract from the action of earlier scenes and would take away some of the recognition scene's dramatic power.

Curculio, a comedy of exchanges

Let's take a look at some diagrams of the exchanges in this play. First, here's how Therapontigonus planned for things to go, as can be seen in Figure 5.2.

Therapontigonus lodged money with Lyco, who was to release it when someone came to him bearing tablets with the soldier's seal. The money, once released, would go to Cappadox, who would then transfer Planesium to the seal-bearer, who would bring her back to Therapontigonus. This would complete what Robert Ketterer has called the play's "circuit of exchange."

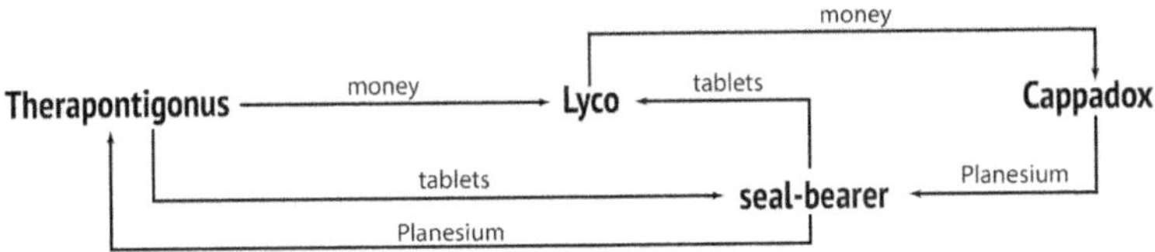

Figure 5.2 The "circuit of exchange" of Plautus' *Curculio*, as originally planned by Therapontigonus. Illustrator, T. H. M. Gellar-Goad.

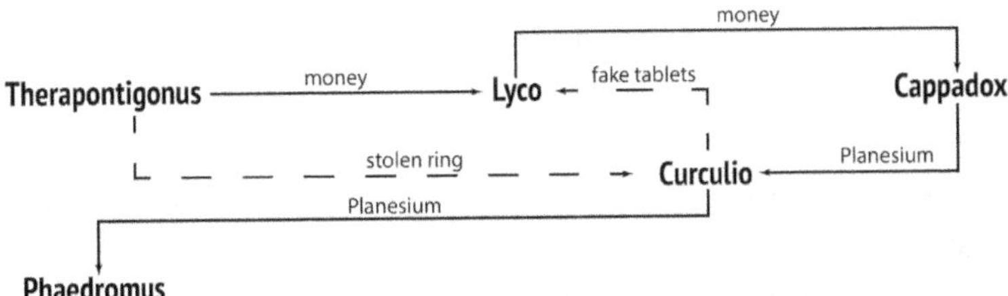

Figure 5.3 The "circuit of exchange" of Plautus' *Curculio*, if Therapontigonus were the ultimate object of the deception plot. Illustrator, T. H. M. Gellar-Goad.

Curculio's tricksy intervention short-circuits the planned exchanges. A hypothetical, alternate-universe version of *Curculio* would make Therapontigonus the ultimate object of Curculio's deception scheme. In this version, he'd never recover his money, and the sex-trafficker would simply receive payment for Planesium and wouldn't end up in any trouble, as illustrated in Figure 5.3.

In this scenario, Therapontigonus loses two things (money and ring) and receives nothing in return, while Phaedromus obtains Planesium (and Curculio the ring) without losing or spending anything. Cappadox receives money in exchange for Planesium. The balance in the theatrical economy has shifted towards the right side of the diagram, and the circuit of exchange is open rather than closed.

Instead, Plautus has chosen to incorporate Therapontigonus into the social network of Planesium and Phaedromus, and thus he has chosen Cappadox rather than the soldier to be the dupe of the play.

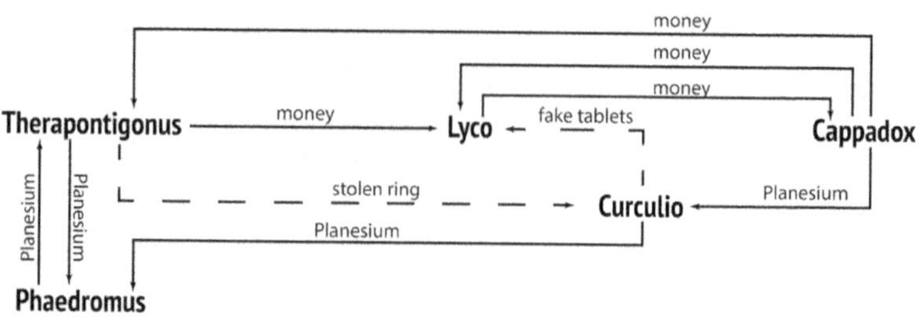

Figure 5.4 The "circuit of exchange" of Plautus' *Curculio*, as it actually happens. Illustrator, T. H. M. Gellar-Goad.

Here's the commerce map of the play as it actually transpires, shown in Figure 5.4.

All the economic resources flow away from Cappadox, and everybody else breaks even or gains something for free. Cappadox loses Planesium, has to give Lyco back the money he received from him, and has to pay the soldier back, too. Curculio will probably end up returning the stolen ring to Therapontigonus, but he's pretty confident he'll secure lots of free meals out of the whole situation anyway (659–65, 675). Phaedromus takes Planesium from Cappadox, but then by advocating for Planesium on the matter of the ring, he facilitates the recognition between her and Therapontigonus, and restores her to him as his sister. Therapontigonus reciprocates by approving of her marriage to Phaedromus, and, in so doing, he transfers her back to Phaedromus' household. Therapontigonus technically "breaks even" in the circuit of exchange, but he actually does better than that, since a byproduct of all the circulation is reunification of his family plus a marriage alliance with Phaedromus' household.

Staging

Just as the text tells us what props show up in *Curculio* and how they're used, so also what the characters say informs what the actors must have done on stage. At the simplest level, when characters use a demonstrative pronoun such as "this" or "that," they are likely also physically pointing at something close to them (this, *hoc*) or farther away (that, *istud/illud*). Similarly, the entrances and exits of characters give a sense of blocking, of who stands where during each scene. It is a standard convention of Roman comedy that one side entrance of the stage leads to the Forum and the other leads out of town, either to the port (as in *Curculio*) or the countryside. The script indicates that Phaedromus' house is next to a shrine of Aesculapius that is, in turn, next to Cappadox' house, which itself has an altar to Venus out front (14, 33, 71). We can visualize the stage layout as shown in Figure 5.5.

Let's look at how a sequence from *Curculio* might be staged. Specifically, I'll start from the scene where Lyco the banker and Therapontigonus the soldier argue (533), through to the finale, with closer analysis of the blocking in the recognition scene between Planesium and Therapontigonus. Here's a rough sketch of how character entrances and exits take place in this sequence, as shown in Figure 5.6.

We start with an empty stage. Therapontigonus and Lyco the banker enter in the middle of a dispute (533, #1). They're coming from the Forum, the business center of the city, where bankers mostly would

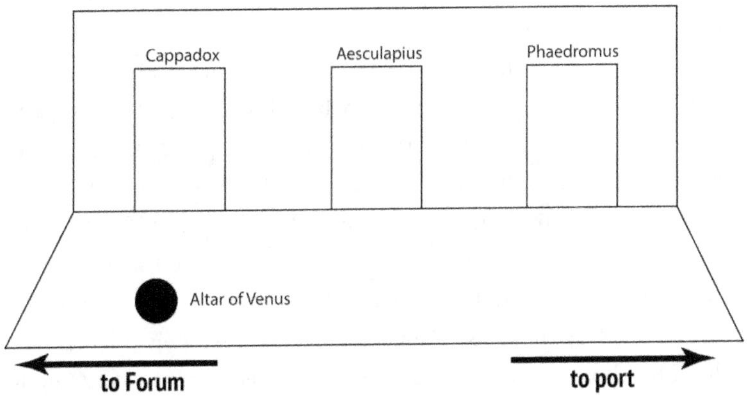

Figure 5.5 The stage layout of Plautus' *Curculio*. Illustrator, T. H. M. Gellar-Goad.

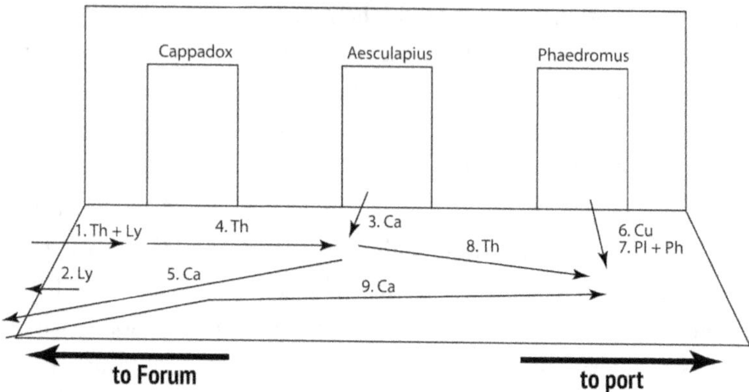

Figure 5.6 A diagram of character movement of the end of Plautus' *Curculio* (lines 533–729). Illustrator, T. H. M. Gellar-Goad.

be—indeed, Curculio locates bankers there during his rant against them in the previous scene (507). After Therapontigonus and Lyco have argued, Lyco leaves, presumably back to the Forum (554, #2). This leaves Therapontigonus at a loss, lingering on stage, with no idea where he should go next (555–6). He is given some guidance when Cappadox the sex-trafficker emerges from the onstage shrine to Aesculapius (557, #3). I know Cappadox is coming on stage by this route because he'd previously told us he'd go into the shrine to offer a thanksgiving sacrifice after successfully concluding—or so he thought—the sale of Planesium (527). Cappadox says he's headed to find Lyco (558–60), so, again, presumably towards the Forum. But, Therapontigonus, seeing Cappadox, goes up to him to start another fight (560, #4). After they've had their argument, Cappadox heads out to find Lyco (588, #5). This once more leaves Therapontigonus at a loss, lingering on stage.

Curculio then enters from Phaedromus' house to complain about Planesium (591, #6). Next Planesium enters, dragging Phaedromus behind her, hot on Curculio's tail (599, #7). Phaedromus catches up to Curculio and physically grabs hold of him (601). Shortly thereafter, Therapontigonus finally notices the commotion going on one door over from him, spots Curculio, goes up to him, and starts another altercation (610, #8). Phaedromus joins in, and the three argue, including some physical activity related to the formalities of legal procedure (621–3) and a couple of punches thrown (624–7).

Planesium intervenes in the totally derailed conversation to refocus the men (628) and ups the stakes of the scene by dropping to her knees and clasping Therapontigonus', in a traditional gesture of supplication, the most desperate of social customs (630). Therapontigonus pulls a typical blowhard-soldier move and brandishes his military gear (632), but subsequently tells Planesium to "stand up" (635) so he can tell her the backstory of his ring. After hearing what he has to say, Planesium tries to embrace him as her own sibling (641), but he pushes her away out of suspicion. Once Planesium has given her own backstory, though, Therapontigonus finally does embrace her as his own sibling (657), allowing her to embrace him back with the exact same words she'd said before (658). The verbatim repetition does a nice job of book-ending the story of Planesium's kidnapping.

After this climactic moment, the play is on a downhill path to the conclusion. Therapontigonus and Phaedromus likely clasp hands or otherwise physically mark their agreement to a wedding between Planesium and Phaedromus (675), and the four characters may be embracing in celebration when Therapontigonus notices the approach of Cappadox (676/678, #9). The sex-trafficker is coming from an encounter with Lyco in the forum with other bankers present (679–85). Cappadox is headed towards his house (685), but Therapontigonus and Curculio interrupt him (lines 685–6) and draw him over to them for the arguments and abuse he'll suffer through until play's end.

Again and again, I have appealed to the text as guide for stage action. Plautus includes in his dialogue almost all the stage direction one would need, either explicitly or by implication. He wasn't doing this for us, obviously, but rather for his actors—some were probably illiterate, so would have had to memorize the script by ear, and couldn't have read blocking instructions slipped between lines of speech. What they learned had to contain most of the cues they would need for what to do in performance (and in reperformance, without Plautus around to direct). For example, the interactions between Palinurus and Phaedromus in the opening scene of *Curculio* give the actors (and us) guidance for how to stage the scene. Palinurus' opening words (1–2) indicate a scene with not just two speaking characters but a whole "entourage" (1) following Phaedromus, who himself is in some sort of outrageous outfit (2). Phaedromus has to be carrying a candle (9). The repeated use of the pointing-word "this" (14, 15) suggests gestural action, with Phaedromus pointing pointedly at the two stage buildings he's telling Palinurus about (so also with the "here"s, 33 and elsewhere throughout the scene).

When Phaedromus greets the door and Palinurus makes fun of him for doing so (16–18), Phaedromus may give the door a familiar salutation traditionally used between humans, with Palinurus parodying Phaedromus' gestures. The testicle pun (30–2) practically begs for some naughty miming to reinforce the *double entendre*. Likewise, when Palinurus asks Phaedromus whether Planesium is still a virgin with the agricultural euphemism, "is she already carrying the yoke?" (50), he probably mimes something sexual, in line with the metaphor of ox-plowing implied by "yoke." Phaedromus is probably trying to act like his nighttime erotic escapades are totally normal, while Palinurus is overacting, to draw attention to what he sees as violations of his traditionalist moral sensibilities.

At 75, the physical action picks up, as Phaedromus says to Palinurus, "hey, slaveboy, gimme the wineskin"—Palinurus has been carrying a wineskin all along. Their subsequent argument over the wineskin (82–7) probably involves lots of brandishing and ogling of it. Thereafter (88–94), the text tells us that Phaedromus adopts the words (and the actions) of a person making a ritual offering, including pouring a libation of wine upon the threshold of Cappadox' door (92), with Palinurus again mocking and parodying Phaedromus' behavior. As the scene ends, they extinguish the candle and retreat, to make room for the grand entrance of Leaena: "shut up, let's conceal the light and our voices" (95).

We've spent a lot of time by now within the play-world of *Curculio*. But there's a whole world outside the play, too, a world inhabited by theatergoers, ancient and modern—and *Curculio* knows it. Chapters 6 and 7 examine how Plautus' metatheater brings spectators into the play and the play out into real life. Chapter 8 makes connections between the play and the historical lives of the inhabitants of ancient Rome.

6

Play Inside and Outside the Play: *Curculio* and Metatheater

Sometimes the people in the movie or show or play don't play by the rules. Sometimes they acknowledge that they're fictional characters. They turn right towards you and talk directly to you. They try to use their awareness of being in a fiction to reshape the story to their advantage. When this happens, the invisible barrier between you and what you're watching—the transparent "**fourth wall**" you've been viewing through—is broken. You can no longer pretend like you are an unseen observer, eavesdropping on their lives.

This phenomenon is a classic example of metatheater, the topic of this chapter. Metatheater is when what you're watching goes meta. It's theater about theater. Plautus wrote long before the advent of film, so he didn't have a **fourth wall to break**—but he *is* one of the most skilled and exuberant users of metatheater. In this chapter, I present an overview of four basic types of metatheater, followed by a survey of minor metatheatrical moments in *Curculio* and then, in chapter 7, a close look at the metatheatrical magnum opus at the center of the play, the Choragus.

Type 1 metatheater in my typology is when there's a play within a play, or a TV show within a TV show. An obvious example of this is Shakespeare's *Hamlet*, where the title character puts on a literal play, with actors and everything, to try to trick his uncle into showing signs of a guilty conscience. In Plautus, the play-within-a-play routine is most common when a character acts as another character, often in disguise. In *Curculio* specifically, we watch Curculio give a virtuoso performance as "Summanus," complete with eyepatch disguise. He fools both Lyco the banker and Cappadox the sex-trafficker with ease. He possibly bamboozles even Therapontigonus the soldier: Therapontigonus has already met Curculio (in the dice-and-drinking backstory Curculio describes at 337–63), and so the soldier knows Curculio to be a freeborn hanger-on, but Therapontigonus suggests near the end of the play that he thinks Curculio (who is maybe still wearing the eyepatch) is an enslaved person (623). This might be a sign that the soldier is confused by the parasite's disguise.

Type 2 metatheater is when a play or movie is about the craft of playwrighting or moviemaking. So, for instance, the ancient Greek comedian Aristophanes' play *Frogs* is a drama with a plot centered on the question of whether Aeschylus or Euripides (both tragedians) was the better dramatist. Plautus' later comedic colleague Terence likes to use the prologues of his plays to express opinions on issues of theatrical style, adaptation techniques, and controversies in the world of acting and producing. The most famous instance of Type 2 metatheater in Plautus is probably this one-liner from the enslaved trickster Chrysalus of *Bacchides*: "even *Epidicus*—a play I love as much as I love myself—I never want *not* to watch it so much as when Pellio is starring in it" (214–15). This low blow to Pellio's acting ability has a character in one Plautine play aware of the existence of another Plautine play!

Type 3 metatheater is when characters acknowledge that they're in a play or TV show or movie. This can come in the form of looking directly at the camera or audience and addressing the viewers. Type 3 metatheater can also show up in dialogue. For instance, a couple of times in Plautus' *Pseudolus* (387–8, 720–1), one character says to another something like, "I'll fill you in later, I'm not gonna repeat myself, the audience has already heard, plays are long enough already." In *Curculio*, Planesium asks Curculio to tell her where his ring came from, the one he stole from the soldier. *We* already know this, Phaedromus does as well, but Planesium hasn't heard it yet. When Phaedromus presses Curculio to tell her, Curculio replies, "I told you already where I got this from. How many times do I have to tell you?" (608–9). This bit of irritation nods at how Curculio here is repeating the important plot point, for the audience's benefit as much as for Planesium's.

Finally, Type 4 metatheater is when a character acts like a producer, director, or playwright. In contrast to Type 1, Type 4 does not actually involve a play within a play. Instead, a character will behave this way metaphorically, by instructing other characters on how they should act or stage-managing them, or by describing a clever scheme in terms of plots, storylines, or fictions. In *Pseudolus*, the title character says he'll behave like a playwright (*poeta*) and invent the cash he needs. And a bit later he directs a sidekick on what to perform during an upcoming scene with his arch-nemesis.

The bulk of metatheater in *Curculio*, besides the Choragus, is Type 3 and Type 4 metatheater, as we'll see in a few moments. The Choragus himself blends all four types. Most clear is Type 3, in his direct address of the audience. His mention of the mechanics of performance represents Type 2. Meanwhile, his tour through the Forum in search of comedic low-lifes combines Type 1 (his monologue is kind of like a comedy within a comedy) with Type 4: he is a stage official, after all, and is directing the audience along the path of his tour.

Type 1 metatheater in *Curculio*

The first kind of metatheater, the play within a play, doesn't appear in full in *Curculio*. There's a vague gesture at it in the language Cappadox uses when seeking an interpretation of his dream: "I'll tell you the story" (246, echoed by the Cook at 256). Perhaps here we could imagine that Cappadox is giving the setup for a small-scale drama of some sort. But the play doesn't dwell on Cappadox' dream, so it doesn't really go anywhere.

Clearer is Curculio's run in disguise in arc 3 of the play. He signals to us that he's putting on a show when he first sees Lyco, with the words,

"I'll pretend like I don't know the guy" (391). In a sense, all scenes in which Curculio is tricking people under the pseudonym Summanus become plays within the play. Lyco, Cappadox, and Therapontigonus are the spectators, and their failure to perceive that they're watching a performance means they easily fall prey to Curculio's schemes.

Perhaps the most interesting bit of Type 1 metatheater in *Curculio* comes towards the end of the play, in Planesium's story of being kidnapped as a child. Her backstory involves theater (643–50):

> She [Planesium's nurse] had taken me to the Dionysia to watch a show. After we'd gotten there, just as she'd set me down, a whirlwind stirs up, it knocks over the whole theater, I get real scared. Then somebody snatches me up—I'm terrified and afraid, I'm neither living nor dead.

Planesium was kidnapped while watching (*spectatum*) a show (*spectacla*) during the festival in honor of Dionysus. Dionysus is the Greek god not only of wine but also of theater—Bacchus is another Greek name for him, the Roman name is actually Liber—and the Dionysia festival in ancient Athens involved performance competitions of drama. So, the spectacle at which Planesium met with misfortune was specifically a theatrical performance.

Moreover, the Dionysia is part of one of the archetypal plots of the Greek genre of New Comedy that Plautus adapts. A disturbingly commonplace backstory to these comedies is that the young woman protagonist was raped, and much of the plot surrounds the identification of the rapist and the resolution of the crisis precipitated by the sexual assault. The standard circumstance for the rape? While the young woman was returning home from a religious festival, often specifically the Dionysia (as in, e.g., Plautus *Cistellaria* 156–9). The mention of the Dionysia receives only a single line in *Curculio*, but it sets up the potential for a *mise-en-abîme* (mirror-reflecting-mirror) situation. It pushes the audience to think about festivals as sites *for* theater, sites *about* theater, and sites within the fictional worlds *of* theater. It's Dionysia all the way down.

Type 2 metatheater in *Curculio*

One way that comedy in particular can import the literary dimensions of theater into its own theatrical world is through **paratragedy**. Paratragedy is parody of tragedy. It's when a comedy makes fun of tragedy by doing an exaggerated or lowbrow version. It can take place with a great deal of specificity—Aristophanes' *Women at the Thesmophoria* parodies Euripides' *Andromeda*, *Helen*, *Palamedes*, and *Telephus*—or it can come in the form of generic riffs on tragic style, tragic situations, and tragic stereotypes.

It is in paratragedy that I see the main piece of Type 2 metatheater in *Curculio*, and it involves the title character. Curculio's tale of his encounter with Therapontigonus (335–63) reads to me like parody of tragic messenger speeches. Your typical Greek tragedy has a momentous turn of events take place during the play—but off stage. The audience learns what's happened only from a messenger, usually a bit character, who describes the events in detail, often gory. So it is with the death of Pentheus in Euripides' *Bacchae*, Heracles'/Hercules' murder of his wife and children in Euripides' *Heracles*, and Heracles' own death in Sophocles' *Women of Trachis*. The messenger speech is a pivotal moment in the tragedy, the signal of the story's tragic turn.

Curculio's arrival and story are likewise pivotal, although they set up a comic deception rather than wrapping up a tragic crisis. His speech begins with heightened emotion: before he even makes it to the main thing, Phaedromus interrupts to say, "you're destroying me with your words!" (335), and Curculio presents himself as feeling "all doom and gloom" (336). Curculio spins a long yarn, with a vivid narrative including direct quotations of conversations he had (342–8, 351–3). Curculio is really playing up the suspense throughout his speech, and once Phaedromus interrupts him to try to move the story along (357), Curculio seems to draw it out even longer.

The paratragedy here could have appeared in the original Greek comedy Plautus has adapted into *Curculio*, if indeed an original existed. It's also possible that this scene is new in Plautus and plays off *Roman* tragedy rather than Greek. Either way, the emotion and staging and tension would, I think, have been obvious enough that an audience would pick up on it as being parodic—just like you might be able to tell when a TV sitcom is making a reference to a famous movie or something, even if you're not familiar with the source for the reference. And we should keep in mind that, even though Curculio's speech takes place in a comedy, the tension and suspense is real for the audience. Curculio's tale could very well have ended tragically for Phaedromus, with no money and no help and no options from Curculio upon his return to town. We wouldn't in that case be dealing with a tragedy, but Curculio's deception plot would have instantly become an order of magnitude harder.

Type 3 metatheater in *Curculio*

Plautus really likes his characters to know that they're characters. A couple moments in *Curculio* feature somebody explicitly or implicitly acknowledging that they're not real but in a play. When Phaedromus tells Palinurus he's making an offering to Venus, and Palinurus deliberately misunderstands him as sacrificing *himself* to Venus, Phaedromus replies, "myself, you, and all these people" (74). As he says, "these people," Phaedromus probably points to the audience, at once **breaking** the illusion that the spectators are flies on the wall and drawing the viewers themselves into the world of the play. Similarly, when Therapontigonus hits Curculio during their legal argument near play's end, Curculio calls out for the help of his fellow citizens (626). This appeal is directed straight out into the crowd; we, the spectators, become citizens of Curculio's Epidaurus, or he of our Rome.

A spectator with an ear for metatheater can detect subtle metatheatrical winks and nods elsewhere in the play. So, for instance, since the action of Plautine comedy almost always takes place within a single day (*Curculio* is unusual, as I noted in Chapter 4, for opening with a nighttime scene), mention of "today" (143, 207) can be understood as meaning "during the plot of this play," while promises to do something "tomorrow" (526, Lyco's guarantee to pay Cappadox what he's owed) come to mean "after this play is over," i.e., never.

Palinurus lectures Phaedromus about which erotic adventures are okay and which aren't. His key recommendation is to stick to the kind of sex objects who won't bring shame to him or his family "if the public finds out" (29; Chapter 2). The characters are on stage in front of a large crowd of spectators, though, so, *of course*, the public will find out! I take Palinurus' words as an acknowledgement that all the romantic infatuations of comedy's lover boys are always already subject to public scrutiny. Palinurus is laying out for Phaedromus two main pathways for young men in Plautus' genre of comedy. First, a relationship that fits elite men's normative values and ends in marriage—as will eventually happen in *Curculio*, after the implausible recognition of Planesium as a citizen, and as happens with the courtship storyline in Menander's Greek play *Dyskolos*. Second, a sexual dalliance that may survive the play, but ultimately can only be a phase in the young citizen man's progress from youth into adulthood, as with lover boys purchasing or freeing enslaved sex-laborers in Plautus' *Pseudolus* and *Asinaria*.

Rome-specific metatheater

A subtype of Type 3 metatheater is particular to cross-cultural adaptations such as Roman *comoedia palliata*. Plautus and Terence are adapting, for performance in Rome, comedies that were written and performed in Greece. As a consequence, they can play on cultural differences between Greece and Rome in their comedies. In so doing, they may not be doing outrageously overt metatheater, but they are winking at meta matters. Plautus plays with the cultural crossover in both directions in *Curculio*, by both inserting Rome-specific references and exaggerating the Greekness of the play.

Though adapted into Latin for a Roman audience, *Curculio* is still notionally set in Greece, and, in fact, has one of the clearest senses of place—Epidaurus specifically—of any play by Plautus. Maybe references to the Forum, Rome's central public space (502, 507), should be taken simply as a translation of the Greek word *agora*, "marketplace," basically the Greek equivalent of the Forum. But the mention of the Capitoline Hill is harder to write off (269). Cappadox is cracking a joke about a lack of room on the Capitoline for all the oathbreakers in town. No good parallel exists in Epidaurus or in Greek city-states generally for Rome's Capitoline Hill, a center of government and religion. Sure, Athens has the Acropolis, and many other city-states had one, too, but they are only rough equivalents at best. The particular content of Cappadox' joke, the bit about oathbreakers, really depends on the fact that the Capitoline was home to a major temple of Jupiter, keeper of oaths.

Another joke in *Curculio* requires Rome-specific location data. Lyco and Curculio are doing some light verbal sparring (400–3):

> **Curculio** Please don't be obstinate with me.
>
> **Lyco** Well, can I have Congress with you if I can't be of Senate with you?
>
> **Curculio** You sure as hell aren't going to have congress with me, and I damn sure don't like your Congress *or* your Senate.

Curculio tells Lyco not to bother him with a word, *incomitiare*, that comes from the name *comitium*, where Roman citizen men assembled to vote on laws and elections. I translated it as "ob-stinate"/"of-Senate." Lyco picks up on the place name and puns on it with a word, *inforare*, that literally means "poke a hole in," but also sounds like it comes from the word *forum*, just like Curculio's came from *comitium*. I translated it as "have Congress with." Lyco's "poke a hole in" is an innuendo, asking Curculio if he can put it in *his* end-o. Curculio's response explains the joke for anybody who didn't catch it right away. Uniquely based on and in Rome, the joke reminds viewers about where they are in real life as they watch the play, and since *Curculio* was probably first performed in the Forum itself (Chapter 7), the joke hits super-close to home.

A final strand of Roman intrusions into the play's Greek setting comes in the form of mentions of Roman law (Chapter 3). Lyco (376),

Cappadox (684, 722), and Therapontigonus (723) all refer to the praetor, chief judicial magistrate in Rome. Lyco and later Cappadox suggest they'd like to use legal proceedings as a way to dodge their creditors. Again, no good parallel exists for this in Greek law, so we're left with a distinctly Roman plot device that blurs the divide between the Epidaurus of Curculio and the Rome of *Curculio*.

Another recurring Roman preoccupation is the legal requirement for witnesses to verify initiation of a lawsuit. To take an offender to court, you would find the person in public, issue a verbal summons, and make sure another citizen witnessed your doing so. This is precisely what occurs in Phaedromus' initial confrontation with Therapontigonus (620–5): Phaedromus summons Therapontigonus, who refuses. Phaedromus then calls on Curculio as a witness. Therapontigonus objects because (as he suggests) Curculio is enslaved, and therefore ineligible to witness. Phaedromus, annoyed, tells Therapontigonus he'll be summoned without a valid witness, *intestatus* (622), a verbal callback to the no-testicles pun Palinurus makes to Curculio at play's beginning (*intestabilis*, 30). The play-ending confrontation between Cappadox and Therapontigonus echoes the legal arguments and castration humor (694–5); in this scene, Cappadox is not only deprived of due process but also of his masculinity. All this procedural wrangling with witnesses and legal formulas may make the characters seem less Greek, and thus less convincing as denizens of their fictional world, but it also makes them seem utterly familiar to Roman viewers.

Metatheatrical jokes about Greekness and about the genre of comedy

At the same time as *Curculio* uses metatheater by adding Roman features to a supposedly Greek setting, the play also underscores its comedy-ness by over-Greekifying its Greeks, in two back-to-back moments at the beginning of Curculio's first monologue. Included in his list of people who need to stay out of his way are numerous Greek officials: *nec strategus nec tirannus quisquam nec agoranomus | nec demarchus nec comarchus* (a general, a tyrant, a market-regulator, a neighborhood leader, a village leader, 285–6). The chances are pretty slim that someone like Curculio would ever actually run into all of those types on his way through town, so this litany of Greek words is really just ratcheting up the "Greek" feel of the scene and the stage—as when you're watching a movie or TV show set in Paris, they *have* to show you the Eiffel Tower. Two lines later, Curculio starts complaining about the people in town more generally, and he describes them as "those damn Greeks with their damn cloaks" (288, a metatheatrical moment familiar to us from Chapter 5).

Curculio also uses the terminology of stock character types for metatheatrical ends. When Palinurus catches sight of Curculio ahead of his first appearance on stage, he describes him as a *parasitus*, Curculio's stock type (277), but also as "running" (*currentem*, 278). The term "running" indicates that Curculio will be playing the part not only of the brown-nosing glutton parasite but also of the *seruus currens*, the enslaved errand-boy, who's always rushing about in a comic hurry—precisely what Curculio's show-stopping first monologue does.

Likewise, Phaedromus initially describes Planesium as "an enslaved young woman" (*ancillula*, 43), and then goes on to say that Cappadox "wants to make her a sex-laborer" (*eam uolt meretricem facere*, 46). Both *ancilla* and *meretrix* are character types in Roman comedy. With these words, Plautus is communicating to us that Planesium not only faces a horrific change of living situation but also a wholesale transformation of stock type. The specter of this transformation—the forced conversion of a most fundamental element of comedic characters' identities—underscores the fragility of and lack of permanency for people's identities in a society organized around the enslavement of human beings.

On a lighter note, Palinurus' injunction to Phaedromus not to do anything "unworthy of yourself or your type" (23) makes me wonder whether *genus*, "type," might here be understood as "stock type." Perhaps Palinurus is begging Phaedromus not to bring shame on Plautine lover boys everywhere. Of course, the stock type of the *adulescens amans* isn't particularly well-known for virtuous or mature upstanding behavior, so with the metatheatrical sense of *genus*, Phaedromus could take Palinurus to mean he should go wild and have a good time, consequences be damned.

In at least one part of *Curculio*, Plautus uses Type 3 metatheater to peek past a major generic taboo. Telling Palinurus about his relationship with Planesium, Phaedromus reassures him that she is a virgin (57–8):

> **Phaedromus** But she's decent and hasn't yet started sleeping with men.
>
> **Palinurus** I'd believe that, if any sex-trafficker could have decency.

"Decent"/"decency," Latin *pudica* and *pudor*, means sexual modesty or sense of shame. For a citizen woman in Rome, it means no sex outside of marriage (before, during, or after). But calling an enslaved sex-laborer *pudica* is a category error, because they are legally ineligible for marriage. That was a right exclusive to citizens. So, Phaedromus' words subtly foreshadow the play's ultimate denouement, that Planesium will be recognized as a citizen and therefore as marriageable. Establishing her *pudor* early on is crucial for the genre of *comoedia palliata*, since if she's already had sex before marriage, even if enslaved and coerced, she becomes unmarriageable, according to the dictates of the Roman patriarchy.

While the rules of the genre require Phaedromus to emphasize Planesium's *pudor*, Palinurus' reply pushes us beyond the taboo. By rejecting the notion that someone who is enslaved by a sex-trafficker can possibly have *pudor*, Palinurus reminds the audience of the grim realities concealed behind the stock characters and plots of Roman comedy. A *uirgo intacta*—an enslaved sex-laborer who has miraculously never had sex—is a highly implausible theatrical fiction. And even without sexual activity, Planesium's mere presence in Cappadox' house/brothel/showroom is a threat to her *pudor*, much more so given how long she has resided there.

The idea behind *pudor* is that the elite men who ran Roman society wanted to be certain that citizen women are producing citizen babies, in a continuation of citizen "bloodlines" (a racially motivated concept then as now, only Romans knew nothing of genes or DNA and thus couldn't weaponize them for their racial formations). So, being completely certain about when, where, and with whom their daughters and sisters and wives had sex was a central preoccupation for elite Roman citizen men. With Palinurus' offhand rejection of Phaedromus' claim that Planesium is a virgin, Plautus has set up a collision course between the comedic stock types of *uirgo intacta* and sex-trafficker, whose profession and whose very archetype both entail maximizing the profit to be gained from the sale for sexual use of said *uirgo intacta* (Chapter 8). Palinurus even gives us Cappadox' stock character type, *leno*, by name.

Type 4 metatheater in *Curculio*

I see two subcategories of Type 4 metatheater in *Curculio*: when characters act like actors, and when they use language of the theater. Most obviously, after he first arrives on stage and fills Phaedromus in on the results of his mission abroad, Curculio announces that he will script for Phaedromus how to forge documents from the soldier for the transfer of Planesium (369–70). Curculio even does some stage-managing, as he directs Phaedromus to make his exit. Earlier, Palinurus played Phaedromus' director, when he told him "you're your very own slave, you're shining a candle so fresh and so clean" (9; Chapter 5). Props make the man. Later in the same scene, when Palinurus lectures Phaedromus that "undercover love is bad" (49), viewers may take "undercover" (*clandestinus*) not only literally but also metatheatrically—it's the kind of love affair that one has while disguised in a costume as a character in a comedy with an erotic plot.

Theatrical language pops up occasionally throughout *Curculio*. Early in the play, Palinurus insults Planesium by calling her an *ebriola persolla*, "drunken munchkin" (192; Chapter 3). The word *persolla* also means "little mask," and thus metatheatrically acknowledges the mask

Planesium's actor wears—and ones the other actors wear, as well. Likewise, at the very beginning of the play, Palinurus asks Phaedromus what's the deal with his outfit (*ornatu*, 2). The word *ornatus* is also the technical term for costume, which means that Palinurus is drawing audience attention to what is probably a pretty outlandish costume that Phaedromus' actor has on.

The Latin noun *ludus* and its related verb *ludo* have lots of senses: "play" as in what kids do, "play" as in theater, "game," "trick," even "school." Any time the word shows up in Plautus, it holds the potential for Type 4 metatheater, often reflecting something about actors themselves or their process of staging a comedy. Let's look at two examples from Curculio's grand entrance. First, Curculio warns Phaedromus not to play around with promises of food: "you'd best not be tricking me" (325–6). But the verb *ludo* here serves as a potent reminder that the food really *is* a trick. They go inside to eat in this play—no onstage banquet scene, like in some other plays of Plautus. So, Curculio, as well as his actor, never actually eats any food.

Second, when narrating his encounter with Therapontigonus the soldier, Curculio says, "he invites me to come play dice [*ut ludam*], so I take off my cloak" (355). By itself, *ludo* in this instance might not activate our metatheatrical senses. But it's followed by a mention of the cloak, *pallium*, that is the hallmark costume element of Plautus' genre, *comoedia palliata*. Maybe we're meant to imagine dice-playing as something actors do backstage, once they've taken off their costumes (their cloaks). Maybe also we can interpret *ut ludam* not only as, "he invites me to play dice," but also as, "he invites me for dice so that I can trick him." Curculio is, after all, about to lay his hands on Therapontigonus' ring, which will be instrumental in pulling off Curculio's big deception plot.

Finally, a couple other words can, I believe, carry metatheatrical weight: *miser* ("poor guy") and *nugae* ("trash" or "trifles" or "blather"). In Roman *comoedia palliata*, lover boys are always whining about how sad and unfortunate (how *miser*) they are that they can't get the girl they want. So, when Cappadox in this play tells Palinurus not to make fun of him by saying, "it's easy to mock a poor guy" (240), he is describing not only a basic avenue of ancient Roman humor—laughing at people less fortunate and less healthy than you—but also a sizable chunk of Plautus' comic routines, built around laughing at a ridiculous, exaggeratedly sad lover boy. With *nugae*, which shows up in the colloquial phrase "you're talking nonsense" (451), we can see another summary of the job of an actor in a comedy. It's an even more compelling bit of metatheater in an interchange towards the end of the play (604):

Planesium You're blathering nonsense.
Curculio I usually do, 'cause that's the easiest way for me to make a living.

This works on three levels. It's a good verbal riposte to Planesium's trash-talking. It also encapsulates the job of the comedic parasite, to flatter and entertain well-off patrons in exchange for food to live by. And it offers a snapshot of what actors do and what Plautus himself does—bring home the bacon by speaking or scripting banter and fictional lines designed to entertain a crowd for a day and no more.

But the main event when it comes to metatheater in *Curculio* is the Choragus.

7

The Speech of the Choragus

The Choragus delivers a surprise monologue about two-thirds of the way through the play (462–86). It's totally unique in ancient Greek and Roman comedy, and it's the part of the play that has attracted the most attention from scholars. After an overview of the speech and a look at the character of the Choragus, we'll walk the path of his tour of Rome, discuss the mechanics of performing the scene, analyze how his speech takes metatheater to new heights, and investigate what all the meta means.

The monologue begins with the Choragus praising how clever Curculio is (462–3), and worrying he might not recover the costumes he lent to the troupe (464–6). He then says that while Curculio's busy inside, he'll give the audience a summary of where to find different kinds of people to meet up with (466–9). At this point, he launches into a list of types of people and locations in central Rome (470–85). In his final line, the Choragus says that the door to Phaedromus' house is opening and that he needs to stop talking (486).

It isn't until the first line of the Choragus' "where to find people" section (470) that Rome is explicitly mentioned (specifically the *comitium*, the site for voting assemblies). Up to that point, the audience has been hearing from a clearly metatheatrical character who is doing some mid-play theater criticism, and talking about costume rental—two metatheatrical acknowledgements that it's not real but a play. But when Rome itself is brought into the speech, the metatheater hits a new level, and the audience would realize they're watching something truly special and unique.

This is the earliest example in Latin literature of a narrative constructed out of references to physical spaces and place. It's the longest passage in Plautus that refers to Rome. It parodies the familiar Roman political activity of a public speech by a statesman, called *officia oratoris* ("orator's duties"). It's also a parody of a genre of literature that would be familiar to Greeks and learned Romans in the audience: didactic, or teaching poetry. And it is marked off as special and different in terms all spectators could understand, because a whole musical segment, a section of trochaic septenarii, is devoted to it (Chapter 4). The monologue of the Choragus is a leading candidate for Plautus' tour de force, because it's unparalleled in any play by him or by any other author from ancient Greece and Rome.

The Choragus as professional and as theatrical character

What is a choragus? I can't say anything with absolute certainty, other than that the choragus was a kind of professional involved in the production of a play at Rome. The Latin word *choragus* is used only twice outside of Plautus in all surviving ancient Roman literature. A few things the choragus seems not to have been: a director, a stage manager, a member of a single acting troupe. The choragus was not like the Greek figure from which the Latin word comes, the *khorēgos*, a wealthy citizen man assigned to finance the production of a play or series of plays, instead of income tax. A primary responsibility of the Roman choragus, by contrast, was providing costumes and props for plays.

The choragus was contracted separately from the playwright and acting troupe. The contract was issued by the aediles in charge of the festival where the play was to be performed. Since the choragus was paid by the aediles, the acting troupe wouldn't have to worry about paying for, storing, or transporting equipment for plays they put on—a welcome bit of assistance for itinerant bands of actors, who might need to travel light and perform plays with wildly different props and costumes. In Rome, the choragus might even have been responsible for building the stage.

Curculio isn't the only time a choragus pops up in Plautus, although it is the most significant. In both *Persa* (159–60) and *Trinummus* (858), characters who are involved in trickery mention the choragus as the source of disguises needed for their schemes. Type 3 metatheater is active here, since the characters are indicating awareness that they're in a play. In the prologue of Plautus' *Captiui* (61–2), the word *choragium*, "choragus-hood," is used to describe terms on which the acting troupe was hired—for a comedy, not a tragedy, in this case.

In *Curculio*, the Choragus is an actual speaking character, not just a one-off reference. But his role within the play is not completely clear. Is he a bit part, a character who comes on, does a weird little speech as a kind of intermission from the action, and then leaves? Or is he one of the silent characters in an earlier scene in the play, who reveals himself to be the Choragus once he's all alone on stage? Does he have a special mask for the Choragus character, or does he come on without a mask (or take off the mask he was wearing while disguised as a non-speaking character)? Maybe he's meant to be a choragus *in Epidaurus*, the setting of the play itself.

Regardless, no character in the play ever speaks with him, nobody is on stage when he speaks, nobody mentions him, and nobody needs costumes from him. Curculio is the only character who wears any sort of disguise, and it's just an eyepatch he pulls out at random, not something he'd previously checked out from the Choragus. It would be an interesting inversion of the normal order of things if our Choragus first appears disguised as a normal character—in a mask and costume borrowed from the real-life choragus—and removes his disguise right before launching into a speech that removes the fictional facade of the play, to examine the real Rome where it is being performed.

The Choragus does have a connection to Curculio. He talks about Curculio in the monologue and presents the monologue as filling space while Curculio is off stage. Curculio is the last person to speak before the Choragus' solo and the first to speak after the Choragus is done. On a deeper level, the Choragus' speech is the twin of Curculio's opening monologue. In that speech, Curculio goes on a rant about sleazy Greeks (280–98), though he's supposed to be a Greek himself; in this one, the

Choragus, a Roman, takes his Roman audience on a tour of Roman sleazebags. The two passages are approximately equal in length, they correspond to one another, and they complement one another. It's even possible to see them as structurally important together:

Before Curculio's speech	279 lines
From Curculio through Choragus	207 lines
After Choragus' speech	243 lines

The play divides roughly into thirds, cutting before and after the two monologues. These thirds in turn roughly match the play's three subplots of "love" story, deception, and recognition.

The Choragus' tour of Rome

The speech of the Choragus walks us through some major sites in the Roman Forum, central meeting place and marketplace of the ancient City. What makes this moment all the more magical is that *Curculio* was itself performed in the Roman Forum. The audience is hearing about locations in the same area of town they're watching the play in, and can probably see most or all of the places the Choragus mentions.

The Roman Forum was in a state of transition at the time of Plautus' *Curculio*. Figure 7.1 shows a reconstruction of how it looked just a little while after the time of the play.

In the twenty-ish years before the play was first put on, Rome had experienced two major fires (213 and 210 BCE), to be followed by another fire as well as an earthquake in the same decade as the play's production (both disasters 192 BCE). Mathias Hanses suggests that the festival at which *Curculio* was performed may even have been held to celebrate the restoration of Forum buildings—perhaps including buildings that appear in the Choragus' monologue. This period was also marked by increasing political competition between elite citizen families, who had become rich off the spoils of the recently won war against Carthage. And what better way to show your family's wealth,

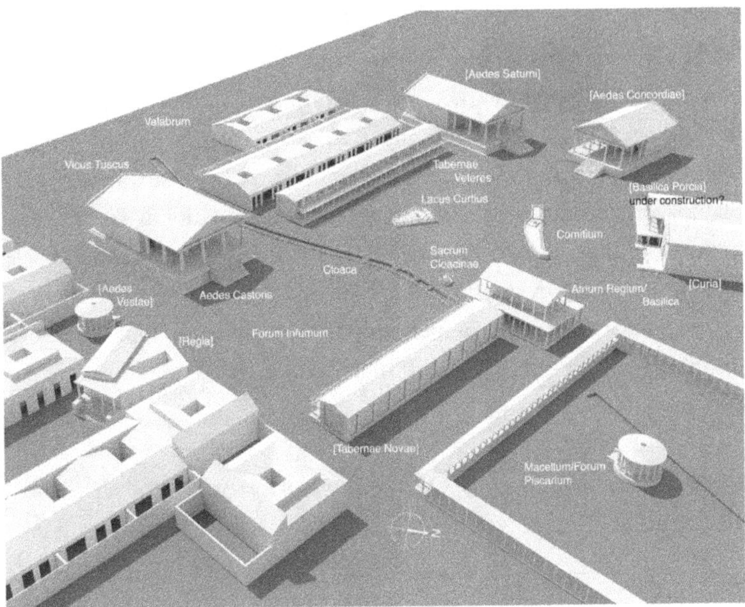

Figure 7.1 The Roman Forum, mid-180s BCE. Sites not mentioned by the Choragus are in brackets. © 2019 Mathias Hanses and Katrin Hanses.

power, influence, and importance than urban development and monumental public works?

As a consequence, when Plautus was composing *Curculio*, his performance space—the Forum—was a bustling construction site with new and improved buildings all around. At the same time, the way the Forum was being developed didn't have a single coherent theme or propaganda message to it, a coherence it would gain 150 years later. The Choragus can imbue the buildings with the meanings and associations he pleases.

An exciting aspect of his speech is that it actually gives scholars some evidence for historical Rome at the time of Plautus, evidence that exists nowhere else. These lines include the oldest surviving reference to the Lacus Curtius in the center of the Forum (477); the earliest description of the shops (*tabernae*) as "the old ones" (*ueteres*, 480), and a specific government building as the *basilica* (472); the most ancient mention of the worship of Venus Cloacina, Venus of the Sewers, in Rome (471); and potentially an older name for what eventually became known as the "meat-market" (*macellum*), here called "Fish Forum" (*forum piscarium*, 474). The mention of a certain person named Leucadia Oppia at 485, meanwhile, appears to be a rare instance in Plautus of naming a real-life, living person, and doing so, the line preserves a little slice of life from Rome at the time, in the name of a woman who was evidently a drain on the finances of married men ("[you'll find] rich men on a spending spree at Leucadia Oppia's house").

Table 7.1 gives the itinerary of the Choragus' jaunt through the Forum.

Table 7.1 The itinerary of the Choragus' tour of the Forum Romanum in Plautus' *Curculio*.

Where	What you'll find	Line(s)
Comitium	Perjurers	470
Sacrum Cloacinae (shrine of Venus Cloacina)	Liars; braggarts	471
Basilica	Wealthy husbands on a spending spree; aged sex-laborers; bargainers	472–3
Forum Piscarium	Potluck dinner-goers	474
Lower part of the Forum	Rich noblemen	475
Middle Forum, near the Canal	Showoffs	476
Lacus Curtius	Chatty, mean smartasses	477–9
Tabernae Veteres ("Old Shops")	Lenders	480
Temple of Castor	Loan sharks	481
Vicus Tuscus	People who sell themselves	482
Velabrum	Bakers; butchers; fortune-tellers; people who transform themselves or others	483–4
Leucadia Oppia's house	Wealthy husbands on a spending spree	485*

* Line 485 repeats most of 472, and so was probably not original to Plautus' premiere performance, but rather used as an alternative in some performance of *Curculio*—possibly long after the premiere, even after Plautus' death.

The Comitium is where the citizens of Rome (men only) would meet to vote on laws and elections. The Cloaca Maxima, the great sewer system of Rome, ran under the Forum, so a shrine to Venus Cloacina, protector-goddess of the sewers, is fitting. It was located near the Comitium. Further in the same direction was the Basilica, a government building that in later times would be used for legal proceedings. At the time of the first performance of *Curculio*, the famous Basilica Aemilia, sponsored by one of the most powerful families in Rome, had not yet been constructed, but the Basilica mentioned by the Choragus may have rested on the same site. It's also possible that the Choragus' "Basilica" actually refers to an entirely different building: the Atrium Regium, or "royal hall," an obscure place-name that may or may not refer to the Regia. The Regia was the building in the Forum that served as the headquarters of the Republic's chief religious magistrate, the Pontifex Maximus.

Around the corner from the Basilica is the Forum Piscarium. From there, the Choragus leaves his initial cluster of sites to move across the Forum towards the Canal, part of the sewer system running right through the Forum's middle. Close by the Canal was the Lacus Curtius, commemorating a Roman legend: a certain mythic young nobleman named Marcus Curtius acted in accordance with a prophecy by mounting a horse in full armor and jumping, horse and all, into an abyss that opened up at this location. (Or maybe when the Choragus mentions the "Lacus," he instead means the Lacus Iuturnae, a pool built near a spring as part of a shrine to the water-nymph goddess Juturna.) From there we jump to the Tabernae Veteres, a complex of permanent stalls that could be rented out for use as shops. One of the more impressive structures in the Forum at that time would have been the Temple of Castor, next on the Choragus' journey. Castor and Pollux were divine twins, sons of Jupiter king of the gods, and they were renowned boxers and horsemen, viewed as divine protectors of everyday people.

From the Temple of Castor, the Choragus heads off to one edge of the Forum, the Vicus Tuscus, "Etruscan Alley." The Etruscans were a people living in Etruria (modern Tuscany), north of Rome. In Roman legend, they had been kings of Rome, until the Romans kicked them out, founded a Republic, and went to war with them. In history, Etruscans were a major cultural-exchange intermediary for Greek influence on Rome. In Plautus' day, Etruscans were a subject people of Rome, known by Romans foremost for their religious knowledge and skill in ritual. The Vicus Tuscus was the Etruscans' neck of the Forum. It was associated also with Vertumnus, a Roman adaptation of an Etruscan god, a divinity of the woodlands and a shapeshifter.

The last stop on the Choragus' tour is the Velabrum, a low-lying area near the Forum that the Vicus Tuscus passed through, and another busy place for commerce. The Velabrum was a major site for building, for gathering, and for political jockeying among the most powerful factions in Rome after the war with Carthage. It was, in other words, one of the most happening places in town. The Choragus uses the word *uel* ("or") a lot in saying who hangs out in the *Vel*abrum—he's punning on the name of the place, like saying "in Orlando you can find theme parks or copyrighted characters or rollercoasters or monorails or merchandising . . ." The tour ends with another pun, as the Choragus tells us the doors (*fores*) are opening, in the very moment his stroll through the *For*um has come to a close.

Figure 7.2 is the same map of the Forum as before, but now with the path of the Choragus' monologue indicated on it, starting at the Comitium on the right side of the map, with the white dot, and meandering around until we arrive at the black dot in the Velabrum at the top left.

Now's a good moment for me to admit that I've begged a question, by calling what the Choragus gives us a "tour." That word implies movement, as does the path that I've drawn on the map above. Scholars before me have tended to treat the Choragus' speech as more like a panorama: he's pointing, they say, to things the audience could see, by craning their head from place to place. That line of interpretation depends on knowing where the audience was seated, and where the stage was built, since a panorama only works if the viewer can take it all

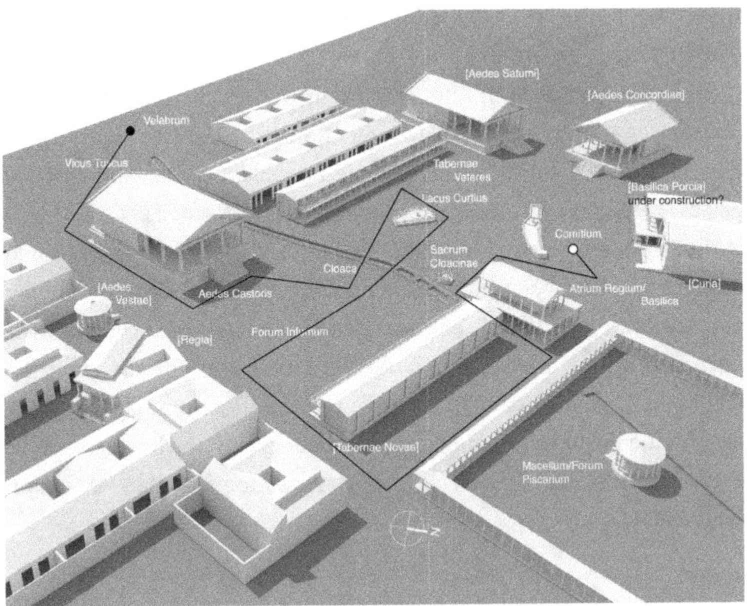

Figure 7.2 The Roman Forum, mid-180s BCE, with the Choragus' itinerary mapped on. © 2019 Mathias Hanses and Katrin Hanses (lines added by T. H. M. Gellar-Goad).

in. Scholars have offered several different conjectures on where it was. For my part, I think it all has to be anchored by the Comitium, since that's where the wealthy apparently had their reserved seats.

But more importantly, I don't think we need to rely so heavily on the exact site of the stage and stands. The Choragus is talking about Rome's downtown during a play performed in Rome to an audience of Rome's denizens. By and large, they're going to know everywhere he's talking about like the back of their hand. Being able to see the exact spots the Choragus is talking about isn't really that important. Everyone will have an easy mental image already, perhaps even from when they were walking in to watch the play. This point is especially pertinent when we recall that most playgoers would be standing, which makes for poor, crowded viewing conditions; and when we remind ourselves that the Romans didn't have corrective lenses to help with difficulty seeing, so some parts of the Forum would have been quite blurry for many people in attendance.

By the same token, it's not important that audience members are themselves standing in the places mentioned by the Choragus, either. For one thing, I don't think that'd be possible, because some of the places are too far apart to be plausible audience areas for a play produced without electronic amplification. For another, most spectators would have no problem envisioning themselves in the places he's talking about, since they'd have been there often in the past, going about their normal downtown business. That's why I've chosen to talk about the Choragus as giving us a tour, instead: viewers can see or imagine a stroll around the Forum they know so well, filled with all the lowlifes they've encountered on their own trips through it *and* the ones they've seen on stage today.

Who's who on the Choragus' tour

Why does the Choragus locate the kinds of people he does in the places he does? In some cases, it's because of a good fit between locale and lowlife, and in others, it's the opposite, a great contrast. In the first column, we find potluck dinner-goers at the Forum Piscarium, a fitting hangout for gluttons; rich noblemen in the lower Forum, near the Via Sacra ("Sacred Way," which at this time was crowded with elite families' mansions); lenders and borrowers at the Tabernae Veteres, a commercial hub; and a crowd of people in the crowded Velabrum. It lay at the edge of the Etruscan quarter (marked by the Vicus Tuscus, Etruscan Alley), so the fortune-teller, *haruspex*, a figure associated by Romans with Etruscan religious knowhow, was an obvious choice. Likewise, a statue of Vertumnus stood in the area along the Vicus Tuscus, which fits the people who transform themselves and others. The "transformation" could refer to human trafficking, in which case it connects to Vertumnus as overseer of commerce; or to the shifting of personal identity, in which case it connects to Vertumnus as shapeshifter and god of social metamorphosis. Etruscans were, to some extent, a marginalized ethnic group in Rome at this point, so it's not unlikely that they might end up holding low-status jobs like baker or butcher, too. The hardest-up among them might have to resort to selling themselves, as do the people that the Choragus says hang out on the Vicus Tuscus.

Matching the five "good-fit" locations on the Choragus' tour are six "contrast" sites. Perjurers are to be found in the Comitium, which is supposed to be the place where Romans make laws, not break oaths. The shrine of Venus of the Sewers is riddled with liars and braggarts, a contrast of human dishonesty with divine purification, of private falsity and public cleanliness. At the Basilica, possibly a seat of civic justice in Rome, we find hagglers, and husbands ready to waste their money (or their wives' money?) on sex-laborers past their prime. The only thing "pure" about the showoffs near the Canal, the major conduit for the sewer system, is their fakery (the Choragus calls them "pure showoffs," 476). The smartasses at the Lacus Curtius behave much differently from the site's legendary namesake, a man of heroic action. Similarly, at the Temple of Castor, a god viewed by the Romans as a helper and guardian, we run into loan sharks—literally, "the kinds of guys you'll immediately regret trusting/giving credit to" (481).

These aren't just generic sleazebags we're encountering as we follow the Choragus around the Forum, though. They're also stock characters from Roman comedy. In Plautine theater, sex-traffickers are stereotypically perjurers, a dead match for the guys the Choragus places in the Comitium. The braggarts (*gloriosi*) at the shrine of Venus immediately call to mind the *miles gloriosus*, the blowhard soldier, of *Curculio* and other plays by Plautus. At the Basilica, the husbands on a shopping spree refer to the horny old man (*senex amator*) of comedy, while the sex-laborers and bankers/bargainers nearby can also be found in Plautus, and in *Curculio* specifically. Cooks, butchers, and fortune tellers, denizens of the Choragus' Velabrum, live in Plautus' comedic towns, too. By the time the Choragus gives them a shoutout, we've already seen a two- or three-in-one on stage, the Cook hired by Phaedromus who gives Cappadox a dream-interpretation (259–72) of the sort an Etruscan *haruspex* (fortune teller) in the Forum might offer.

We end up with what Marcela Alejandra Suárez has called the "Forum Plautinum": part Forum of Rome, part Forum of Plautus' comedies. Lines are blurred between reality and comedy in multiple directions. A fictional character talks to a real audience and invites them to look for theatrical characters in real places they can see around them. The comedy is bursting off the stage and into the City, at the same time as the real world is bursting on stage to take over the comedy (for the duration of the Choragus' speech). And the play's text creates and preserves a specific portrait of the historical Forum Romanum, a Plautine memory of the civic arena, to be performed and imagined by actors and spectators and readers ancient and modern.

Why this monologue?

The speech is an inspired magnum opus of comedy. It draws on the audience's surroundings, something immediate and familiar and shared. It pushes limits by putting disreputable characters into the vicinity of the performance, in some of the most respectable places in Rome—and into spots spectators themselves may have been watching from. The tour of Rome is a tour de force.

The Choragus' speech also connects to other parts of *Curculio*, as well as forging links between the world of the play and the world outside it. Rome's landscape appears not only in this speech, but also twice before it. When the Cook tells Cappadox he should be praying to Jupiter the oath-keeper rather than Aesculapius the healer, Cappadox replies, "if everyone who'd broken oaths wanted to do an overnight ritual [to Jupiter], there wouldn't be enough space available on the Capitolium" (268–9, Chapter 6). The Capitolium was the most important of the Seven Hills of Rome, and was the site of the Temple of Jupiter Optimus Maximus ("the best and the greatest"). The joke here is that Rome itself, like the Epidaurus of Cappadox and Curculio, is overcrowded with cheats and liars. Later, when Lyco the banker is making fun of Curculio's missing eye (this is while Curculio is disguised as "Summanus"), they exchange Rome-related puns and barbs about the Comitium, the Forum, and sexual penetration (400–3, again Chapter 6).

These references to the City are specific to Rome. They're too particular to be mere translations or analogies for something in the Greek original. They remind the audience of their physical location and thus prime us for the Choragus' deeper, metatheatrical delve into Rome. His appearance in the play breaks and blurs the boundaries between fictional Epidaurus and actual Rome. He enters with commentary on Curculio's trickster skills, which suggest he's been watching the play, a spectator like us. But he's also a character within the play—but, then again, his character is a theatrical technician, someone who belongs backstage, not on stage or in the audience. The Choragus asks spectators to notice, and to find comedic character types, in the real-world locations in Rome they're supposed to be pretending aren't there, since the play is telling them to pretend they're watching something unfold in Epidaurus.

Epidaurus is home not only to a major healing center of Asklepios but also to an important Greek theater, one still in use today, as shown in Figure 7.3. Perhaps the Choragus is meant to be the choragus for that theater. In that case, we could wonder whether he's watching a spectacle in Rome or in Epidaurus—and maybe the Rome he's telling us about is as fictional to him as Epidaurus is to us.

All this metatheatrical business is a lot to take in, and it's doing a lot of work in the play. The Choragus, as he stands on stage doing his stand-up routine, may be near the Lacus Curtius, where he locates chatty windbags. If so, it's a nice moment of self-aware self-mockery. Regardless, two main motifs lurk behind his tour of Rome: politics and sex-labor. The whole passage could fairly be described as a political satire, one of the earliest pieces of political satire surviving from ancient Rome. It's not just average people or everyday life being mocked here, but elites and their core values. For instance, seats may have been reserved for

Figure 7.3 The theater of Epidaurus. Photo by T. H. M. Gellar-Goad, 2019.

senators and their families in the Comitium, exactly where the Choragus says you'll find oath-breakers. The untrustworthy men hanging out at the Temple of Castor may be *equites*, the wealthy non-political bigwigs of ancient Rome, placed by the Choragus at the Temple because of an annual procession of equites that passed by there. The contrasts hint at modern Romans not living up to the greater generations of ancestors who built the Forum's monuments.

At the same time, as Amy Richlin notes, the Choragus' Rome features a perhaps-surprising number of sex-laborers. We find them near the Basilica and in the Vicus Tuscus. They are possibly being trafficked in the Velabrum (484), or these men might be engaged as free or unfree sex-laborers. The line at the end about Leucadia Oppia—a woman not attested elsewhere in surviving Roman texts—perhaps refers to a particularly renowned sex-laborer at some point in Rome, or a successful brothel-keeper. The recurrent presence of sexual labor in what the Choragus shows us of Rome may be mainly about comedy, since much of Plautus' theater revolves around sex-laborers, either as desired objects or clever tricksters or long-lost citizens or some combination. Or maybe it's another metatheatrical moment, acknowledging that actors and sex-laborers were not very different in their occupations: sex-laborers, like actors, have to put on a show and conceal what's going on behind the scenes, while actors, like sex-laborers, are dependent upon pleasing the crowd.

The Choragus' Forum is filled with sleazebags—but why? In part, it reflects the comedy in which the Choragus appears. Curculio is a liar and a thief. In his triumph, he turns out to be just like the targets of the Choragus' satire. On a deeper level, though, as Timothy J. Moore has argued, the Choragus seems to be questioning one of the core values of the ancient Roman patriarchal elite: *fides*, "trustworthiness." Throughout the play, but especially in the behaviors of Curculio, Lyco, and Cappadox, it is clear that nobody is to be trusted in Plautus' version of Epidaurus. Then the Choragus ties untrustworthy Epidaurus with Rome, in a speech that blurs the boundaries between theater and real life, and that situates the hucksters of comedy in the real-life Forum. Audiences wouldn't be off-base if they came away from *Curculio* a little less confident in the civic credibility they could count on from their fellow citizens.

One of comedy's superpowers is that it can hold up a mirror to our lives, our societies, and ourselves. Plautus uses metatheater to hold up a mirror to the mirror of comedy, and what we end up with is a funhouse *mise-en-abîme*. The theatrical fiction acknowledges its fictionality to the audience, and in doing so, it draws the audience *into* the world of theater. Or/and: the comedy brings Rome and Roman society into itself, with the result that the audience can reinterpret Rome itself as a comedic set. Nobody in Roman comedy does metatheater like the Choragus does: a behind-the-scenes worker jumps into the scene in order to demolish the pretense that it's anything other than a scene—and then goes around town in real life, pointing out all the scenes already on display.

Something about Plautus made him fascinated by metatheater. It's not unique to him; meta can be found in the other major surviving playwright of Roman comedy, Terence, and all across Roman and Greek literature. For Plautus in particular, though, attention to the processes of comedy emphasizes the similarity between playwright and star trickster, between the deception plot within the play and the deceptive act of acting the play out. And Plautus' bending, breaking, and obliterating the divisions between actors and audience pushes his viewers to think about the performances and dramas that they encounter and are involved in themselves.

8

Curculio and Roman Life

Comedy reflects actual lived experience. The reflection may be like in a funhouse mirror, distorted and strange and hard to believe. But that core of real life, and usually of daily life, is still there, waiting for us to recognize it. Or to recover it. Objects in that mirror may be closer than they appear.

Plautus isn't just an expert jokester and cleverly plotting playwright. He's also a valuable source of information on what life might have been like in the Rome, where he lived and wrote. The fact that his comedies feature everyday situations and non-elite characters gives us a window onto ancient Roman lived experiences that aren't described in other texts and art and monuments that survive from Roman antiquity.

We have to handle Plautus with care, though. He's not an objective reporter. He's going for laughs. But a lot can be gained by reading Plautus with an eye for social history, the stories of past cultures that don't revolve around wars or governments or large-scale movements. This chapter will look at a few categories of ancient Roman daily life: enslavement and sex-labor; food insecurity, poverty, and low-status work; and religious practices. Knowing about Roman customs in each category helps us better understand what's going on in *Curculio*, and examining *Curculio* gives us special insights into the phenomena of Roman culture.

Enslavement and sex-labor

Plautine comedy is theater by and about enslaved persons. At least some of the actors themselves were enslaved, and the stars of most of

Plautus' surviving plays are enslaved characters. Even in a play like *Curculio*, whose title character is a freeborn citizen, enslavement is a preoccupation, with Palinurus trying to play the enslaved clever trickster, Planesium seeking liberation from enslavement, and Curculio disguising himself as "Summanus," a man supposedly formerly enslaved by the soldier Therapontigonus. Each of Plautus' twenty-and-a-half surviving plays includes at least one enslaved character. Jokes about the torture of enslaved persons, often from the perspective *of* enslaved persons, are a frequent element of Plautus' humor.

Rome was an enslaving society. By 201 BCE, the end of the second war with Carthage, the number of persons enslaved in Rome far outnumbered the number of citizens. Rome's economy was built on enslavement. *Curculio*, therefore, is the product of an enslaving society, and we can see as much in how it represents everyday life and interactions. Phaedromus starts the play off by entering with a veritable entourage of enslaved attendants following him. He repeatedly abuses or threatens to abuse Palinurus physically (132; an extended assault sequence at 193–9) and verbally (7, 45, 130). Palinurus and Phaedromus live two doors down from Cappadox, a human trafficker, a man whose job is enslavement. Leaena, the doorkeeper enslaved to his household, has a craving for wine that is played up for laughs on stage, but it's also a glimpse of one of the many cruelties of a life enslaved: to deal with the physical and emotional traumas to which she has been subjected, Leaena self-medicates with alcohol, which leads to addiction and further trauma.

Much of the play's action is predicated on trafficking Planesium. Therapontigonus and Lyco are involved in the sale of a human being. Phaedromus is complicit in the trafficking, and only becomes indignant about Planesium's enslavement when he figures out she wasn't born into it but was born free (608). Curculio, meanwhile, will disguise himself as someone formerly enslaved (413)—but the moment somebody suggests he is, in fact, enslaved, he responds swiftly and with violence (624/625, furthermore using *liber*, a term meaning freeborn, as opposed to *libertus*, freed). Even the suggestion of a status lower than you possess can pose an existential threat to your identity and standing. Within

Plautus' *comoedia palliata*, Curculio is perhaps doubly at risk, since he is fulfilling the trickster role that in many other plays is performed by an enslaved person, the *seruus callidus*.

Curculio grapples extensively with sex-slavery. Planesium is enslaved to a sex-trafficker, although her character type, *uirgo intacta* (freeborn citizen girl wrongfully enslaved), means that she has, miraculously and implausibly, been spared from coercive sexual labor so far. This point is insisted on by multiple characters in the play (57–60, 518, 698). It has to be this way, because if she weren't a virgin, she would, according to the sexist ideologies of the patriarchal elite, be unmarriageable. One reason why she might plausibly be a virgin, despite living in a sex-trafficker's household since youth: Cappadox might be keeping her "pristine" to try to extract a higher price for her when he sells her.

Another term for Planesium's character type, *pseudo-meretrix*, means "sex-laborer but not really." Planesium is technically in the status of an enslaved *meretrix* (sex-laborer), but she has never had sex and so is not a practicing sex-laborer. In ancient Rome, the term *meretrix* literally meant "woman wage-earner" and designated several different categories of sex-laborers. One category of *meretrices* encompassed those who, like Planesium, were enslaved to a sex-trafficker with plans to sell them off to a buyer in a one-time transaction. Others were enslaved in a brothel, still others enslaved and forced to serve as streetwalking prostitutes.

A final category consists of free *meretrices*: non-citizens, often immigrants, who turned to sex-labor to feed themselves. Although free *meretrices* were not subject to the oppressive abuses of enslavers, they were nevertheless still in a vulnerable position in their society, because they did low-status work and lacked legal rights or protection. As a result, they would often need to seek the patronage or goodwill of well-to-do citizen men.

Planesium begins the play enslaved to Cappadox and contracted for sale to Therapontigonus. But without the impossible luck of finding her long-lost brother to prove she was born free, she could have ended up in any of the other categories of *meretrix*. In this alternate universe, if

Phaedromus had bought her, he may have freed her, but he could never have married her, and eventually would have broken things off with her in order to marry a citizen and make babies. This would likely relegate Planesium to the position of a free *meretrix*, dependent upon sex-labor to survive without a regular, committed client. If Therapontigonus bought her, or if Phaedromus did but didn't free her, each would likely tire of her eventually and either reduce her to the menial tasks of enslaved domestic laborers, or would have sold her off to another sex-trafficker (or even back to Cappadox himself—at a reduced price, of course). If neither sale had gone through, she would be left with Cappadox, who might have decided that she was not enough of a luxury commodity to sell at a high price. He would then have forced her into the brothel or streetwalking prostitution, a fate threatened or implied against enslaved sex-laborers in Plautus' *Pseudolus*, his *Rudens*, and the late Roman novel of Apollonius King of Tyre.

Planesium's backstory and possible future, as well as Curculio's strong reaction to the insinuation that he's enslaved, testify to the fragility of freedom in a culture of enslavement. If it weren't for a whirlwind all those years ago, Planesium would never have been kidnapped and enslaved. If he changes his name and his outfit even just a little, Curculio can be mistaken for a currently or formerly enslaved person. These status threats are not mere theatrical fictions particular to the world of the play. The audience of *Curculio* would have included people enslaved and formerly enslaved, people who had been kidnapped by slavers or born into enslavement or taken as war captives in Roman conquests. And Roman citizens in the audience, some of them enslaving people in their own household and some not, would all be aware that Romans abroad could also be captured, kidnapped, or taken in battle and sold into enslavement elsewhere in the Mediterranean. Another of Plautus' plays, *Captiui* ("The Captives"), deals with this issue more explicitly—but it lurks behind every one of Plautus' plays, including *Curculio*, because all of his plays, including *Curculio*, reflect ancient Mediterranean realities and inequities by depicting enslavement and enslaved persons.

Food and hunger

The figure of Curculio himself touches on another of these topics where it's played up for laughs but conceals a more serious concern underneath. Curculio, as a parasite, is a hanger-on and a glutton. He's willing to do whatever it takes to glean a free meal off Phaedromus. But there's no such thing as a free lunch. Curculio has to go abroad on an erotic fool's errand for Phaedromus—in a world where overseas travel is long, uncomfortable, and easily fatal. Curculio, like all parasites in Plautus, is so desperate for a feast that he'll take on any task, no matter how challenging or humiliating.

One obvious point we can make here is that the comedic version of Curculio—the glutton—veils a darker real-world anxiety. Food insecurity, hunger, and malnutrition are simple facts of life for non-elites in the ancient Mediterranean. In Athens, in Rome, and across the ancient world, many people couldn't consistently know how or when they'd have their next meal. (Don't think it's so different now: in the city where I live, Winston-Salem, North Carolina, almost one in five people experience food insecurity, and almost one in four children do.) In the City of Rome at the time of Plautus, thousands of people, both citizens and non-citizens, lived in poverty, and during food-shortage crises (as during wartime) they could be dependent on government distributions of imported grain. Behind the mask of the parasite lies a figure familiar to Plautus' audience, someone driven by the specter of starvation to undesirable labor for a well-off family.

Connected to this subtext is the Roman practice of patron-client relations. Wealthy Roman citizen men would act as a patron for poor Roman citizen men—they'd provide food, money, and legal representation. In exchange, the poor men would serve as clients subservient to their patron, who might require them to run errands, or vote the way the patron wants, or join the patron's gang to intimidate or beat up clients of a rival bigwig. It seems like Curculio is Phaedromus' client, and what Curculio does at Phaedromus' behest, particularly disguising himself as a freedperson to trick Lyco and Cappadox, marks

Curculio's low social status in a way neither he nor the audience can forget.

Poverty and the Roman underclass

Curculio plays the part of Summanus and so is of low status: both of these traits are ones he shares in common with the actor portraying him on stage. The actor was likely enslaved, and while Curculio is free, Phaedromus talks about ordering him around almost as if Curculio is enslaved by him ("I've sent *my* hanger-on to Caria to beg my buddy for a cash loan," 67–8). The audience also learns that Curculio is poor from how he talks about his paycheck-to-paycheck livelihood: "I've got nothing to my name, 'cause what I had I used up real quick" (600). When Curculio tells Phaedromus that they'll be forging documents using Therapontigonus' stolen ring ("I'll tell you how to write," 370), the way he phrases it suggests that he himself cannot write (Chapter 5). Curculio is, like a large proportion of non-elite people living in Plautus' Rome, illiterate.

Cappadox the sex-trafficker, Lyco the banker, and the unnamed Cook are all involved in professions that bourgeois Roman citizens scorn. Sex-trafficking, though legal, was universally reviled by the Roman elite—even as they made ample use of the sex-labor that such trafficking made possible—and sex-trade was often left to non-citizens to handle. Cappadox' name suggests that he is not Roman but from Cappadocia.

Wealthy Romans, like aristocrats in many times and cultures, held moneychanging and banking in disdain, even as they were often necessarily dependent upon it. Elite Romans tended to say honorable men spent their time on governing, the military, farming (well, possessing agricultural forced-labor camps run by enslaved persons), and intellectual pursuits—not merchantry or money-handling. Lyco, then, is also on the outs with the hoity-toity in the audience. You can witness the distaste current in Rome for the two trades in Curculio's rants against Cappadox and Lyco for their professions (494–511).

The Cook, despite his high opinion of himself, is not some revered expert, but in essence a hireling. Sometimes in Plautus the cooks are in fact enslaved characters. In *Curculio*, the Cook seems to be about on par with Palinurus, enslaved in Phaedromus' household, and another member of the play's social underclass. Leaena and Planesium round out the roster, two more people enslaved and consigned to labor, the one menial and the other sexual.

The only characters not on this list are Phaedromus, Therapontigonus, and the Choragus—and the last of those three might also be low-status, tainted by being involved in the theater business, another profession that Roman elites scorned. With *Curculio*, Plautus has decided to present a play featuring the lower classes, in contrast to the focus on well-to-do citizen families in the Greek comedies he adapts. Without Phaedromus' parents around to worry about his moral development, the marriage at the end is kind of a surprise, and the play remains mostly focused on trafficking Planesium, with all the hijinx and wrangling it entails.

Putting Rome's (or Epidaurus') underclass onto center stage allows Plautus to shine a spotlight on the shady parts of Roman society, the unseemly and oppressed underbelly that the upper echelons exploit to maintain their own comfort and privilege. This take is confirmed by the speech of the Choragus, who links Plautus' theatrical exposé of the Roman down-below with a revelatory tour through the exact public space in which the audience has gathered to watch the play. I'm not suggesting that Plautus is calling for a Marxist revolution, but he is, I believe, confronting elites in his audience with depictions of social realities that many would rather ignore. At the same time, he's giving onstage representation to people who perhaps wouldn't often see themselves in public works or public art.

Religious practices

Viewers of *Curculio* are reminded of the performance context of a religious festival by the mention of the Dionysia, another religious festival featuring theatrical performances, in Planesium's tale of being kidnapped (644/645). Outside the play, the context is one of religious observance and celebration, and the public buildings of the Forum that surround the performance space include shrines and temples (such as the Temple of Castor, name-checked by the Choragus, 481). Within the play, too, much religious activity takes place, more so than in most comedies by Plautus or his later contemporary Terence. The ritual and theological elements of *Curculio* are not always mere jokes. By focusing on what this play says about religion, we can examine some forms of individual, personal religious experience apart from the public and state religions that are well-documented in other ancient sources.

The religious theme begins even before Palinurus and Phaedromus first walk on stage, because the set includes a stage door representing the entrance to a shrine of Aesculapius the healing god (mentioned at 14, 204, 699), and an altar to Venus, goddess of love, in front of Cappadox' door (71). Aesculapius' shrine door would probably be decorated with symbols of his worship, so it would clearly be his site. He's the right choice for a play set in Epidaurus, most famous in antiquity for its sanctuary of Asklepios. The onstage shrine, a single "building" within the fictional world of the theater, is probably not meant to be the giant temple complex in Epidaurus where Romans and Greeks and others of Plautus' time could go for a one-stop medico-religious resort. Instead, this is meant to represent an average street in Epidaurus, almost like the whole city is an Aesculapius theme park.

Curculio isn't a medical story, though, it's a "love" story, at least in part (Chapter 2). Besides the altar to Venus, theater-goers hear at the very beginning of the play a mention of her plus Cupido and Amor, "desire" and "love," two divinities associated with Venus. (The Romans liked to take abstract concepts and make divine personifications of them—gods and goddesses embodying the ideas.) The early scene where Phaedromus and Palinurus encounter Leaena and Planesium is filled with Venereal moments, including Leaena's offering of a libation to Venus (125–7), a legal/religious erotic metaphor of "the summons of Venus" (162), two references to the *peruigilium Veneris* (an all-night vigil in honor of Venus: 181, 196), and a reference to Planesium as "my Venus" by Phaedromus (192). Note also this Venus-involved joke-off between Palinurus and Phaedromus (72–4):

Phaedromus I've vowed I'll provide Venus' breakfast.
Palinurus Hmm? You're gonna feed yourself to Venus for breakfast?
Phaedromus Me, you, and [*gesturing to audience*] all these people here.
Palinurus Then you've got a verve for Venus to vomit.

After this scene, Venus fades into the background. But her altar remains on stage through the end of the play. And the Choragus, near the start of his tour of the Forum, directs the audience's attention to the nearby shrine of Venus Cloacina (471), purifier of Rome's water system.

Religious ritual

The back-and-forth between Venus and Aesculapius involves religious ritual. Greek and Roman religion was less wrapped up in concerns of orthodoxy—whether you have the "correct" beliefs, like that Jesus is your lord and savior—and more about orthopraxy, doing the right practices in the right way. What made someone a member of the religious community was not whether they were a believer, but whether they were a *practitioner*. In *Curculio*, Venus receives ritual offerings from Phaedromus (71–4) and Leaena (125–7). Leaena herself receives a sort-of libation from Phaedromus (80–1 and 92), and she parodies libations when she pours water on the hinge of Cappadox' door to keep it from creaking (160). The purpose of all these offerings is to propitiate their divine (or mortal-treated-like-divine, or door-treated-like-divine) recipients, to make the recipients favorable to the person making the offering. Phaedromus needs to feel like Venus is on his side if he's going to achieve erotic success—but, more pragmatically, he also needs

Leaena on his side if he wants a chance to see Planesium. His offering to Leaena is successful not only because she helps Phaedromus out but also because she says that, for her, the wine is like incense (*stacta*, 102), another standard ritual offering in ancient Greece and Rome.

When it comes to Aesculapius, the main ritual event is "incubation": spending the night sleeping in his shrine in hopes of being healed, or of receiving a propitious dream that will show the path to healing. This is precisely what Cappadox the unwell sex-trafficker is doing on the night the play begins (61–2). He does obtain a dream from his incubation, and then seeks out another ritual, a dream-interpretation (*coniectura*, 245–50, 253–73).

Later in the play, when Lyco first appears on stage, before he even speaks a word of dialogue, he does a formal ritual greeting (*salutatio*) of Aesculapius at the entrance to the shrine (389–90). Curculio, who spots him doing it, says his head is covered (389). This is not incidental detail, but a key component of Roman ritual practice: when Romans were engaged in religious rites, they covered their heads. The phrase, "with head covered," is used twice earlier in *Curculio*, during the title character's first monologue, in a rant about Greeks (288, 293). In that context, Curculio may simply be saying the Greeks look shady because they are trying to keep their faces hidden. More likely, he could be hitting the Greeks for being too eager to do religion all the time, or being ostentatious about it when they do it.

The Choragus makes mention of a particular ritual official in his tour of the Forum: a *haruspex* (483). The *haruspices* were Etruscan experts who practiced haruspicy, the inspection of entrails. Someone undertaking an animal sacrifice could hire a *haruspex* to inspect the liver and other internal organs of the sacrificial victim after it was slaughtered. The *haruspex* would identify any special markings or irregularities, and interpret their religious or prophetic significance. In *Curculio*, the *haruspex* is one of the hirelings crowding the Velabrum in the Etruscan Quarter. Haruspicy is a job the Romans outsource to Etruscans, because they have a tradition of expertise in this sort of religious ritual.

Gods

Romans—and Greeks, too—were totally okay with adding new gods to their pantheon. When Romans were conquering a new town or in times of crisis, they might import a foreign deity to signify their victory or salvation. So, it's fun and noteworthy, but not sacrilegious, when characters in Plautus compare themselves or other people to gods. Phaedromus, when he sees Planesium on his nighttime visit, wastes no time in calling himself and then her divine: "I'm a god . . . what have you ever seen or ever will that's more godlike [than her]?" (167–8). Curculio later calls Phaedromus his Genius, "guardian spirit" (301), and Phaedromus in turn calls Planesium *his* Genius (628); Phaedromus calls Curculio his Opportunitas (305), a divine personification sort of like "Mr. Right Time, Right Place." The name Curculio chooses for himself, Summanus, was the name of a Roman god, but one not well understood nowadays and not even by some Romans of later periods. He might be the god of nighttime thunder—and, if so, that makes for a good namesake for a trickster who wreaks havoc under cover.

Characters also associate themselves with the divine through patron deities. Liber, the Roman god of wine, is an obvious choice for Leaena, and he's mentioned twice in connection with her (99, 116). Curculio refers to Hercules as his "nurse" (*nutrix*, 358)—a great patron for Curculio, because Hercules had a huge appetite, especially in Greek comedy, and possibly some cross-gender humor, since *nutrix* is a feminine noun. Planesium calls upon the divine personification of her loyalty to her family, her Pietas (639–40), when she is finally reunited with Therapontigonus. Behind the jokes and the drama is evidence for people feeling personal connections to individual gods in their daily lives.

Language

Religious language in *Curculio* takes the form of oaths, curses, a vow, a prayer, an invocation, a blessing, and some words peculiar to Roman religion. By paying attention to how Plautus uses religious language, we can glean a sense of how the denizens of Rome in his time likely talked about religion, in ways both serious and playful, both familiar and foreign to our own societies' conversational uses of religious concepts and terminology.

The gods figure mundanely into the everyday speech of Plautine comedy, in oaths like "for Pete's sake" or "goddammit," with almost content-less emphasis. In Plautus, three common oaths involve gods:

pol/edepol (Pollux, demigod, twin of Castor)
castor/ecastor (Castor, demigod, twin of Pollux)
hercle/hercule/mehercle/mehercule (Hercules)

The first is used by both men and women characters, the second only by women, and the third only by men. Surprisingly, neither of the women characters of *Curculio*, neither Leaena nor Planesium, uses *castor*, even though the Choragus will mention the Temple of Castor looming over the Forum, where the play is being performed. Leaena uses *pol* once (135), and Planesium doesn't swear at all. All of the men characters do swear, with the exception of the Cook (a total of 20 uses of *hercle* and 9 of *edepol* across the play).

Oaths—ones that are much more deliberate than the default *edepol* or *mehercle* so common in comedy, and represent a strong invocation of divine authority for a particular statement—can be used to express surprise, shock, or outrage, such as when Palinurus, catching sight of Curculio in the distance ahead of his first appearance, shouts "by the immortal gods!" (*pro di immortales*, 274). At the end of the play, as Cappadox is seized by Therapontigonus, the sex-trafficker appeals to "the trustworthiness of the gods and mortals" (*pro deum atque hominum fidem!*, 694). With these words, Cappadox protests the due-process violation that Therapontigonus is committing, since he has not formally summoned Cappadox to court. The surprise reunion between sister and brother prompts an identical oath from each, Planesium at the start of the recognition scene and Therapontigonus at its end ("by Jupiter!," *pro Iuppiter*: 638, 655).

Oaths also can help intensify claims that characters make. Phaedromus does this twice, early in the play. First, he protests to

Palinurus that, contrary to Palinurus' fears, his love object Planesium is not a marriageable or married citizen woman: "and may Jupiter over there never allow me!" (27). Phaedromus' "over there" may indicate that the actor playing Phaedromus is gesturing beyond the stage in the direction of the Temple of Jupiter, keeper of oaths, on the nearby Capitoline Hill. Later, promising to Planesium that he will somehow purchase Planesium's freedom, Phaedromus shows he's serious by saying "so help me Venus" (208). This is a fitting divinity for Phaedromus to appeal to, given that he's making an erotic promise as part of an erotic storyline while standing near an altar consecrated to Venus.

The flipside of oaths is curses, four of which appear in *Curculio*. When Palinurus defeats him in a bout of banter, Phaedromus says the equivalent of "go to hell": "may the gods do you ill" (130). Palinurus does something similar when Curculio out-banters *him* ("may Jupiter and the rest of the gods destroy you!," 317), and Phaedromus repeats Palinurus almost exactly to curse Therapontigonus for not complying with his legal summons (622). Once Cappadox discovers that Phaedromus was not a neutral party at the time he offered to serve as arbiter between Cappadox and Therapontigonus, the sex-trafficker hurls another imprecation of this sort against Phaedromus (720). When men in this play are bested, either in verbal jousts or legal wrangling, their last resort is to hope the gods will damn their opponents.

The nighttime sequence at the opening of *Curculio* is a hotbed for religious speech. Palinurus encourages Phaedromus to greet the gods formally (70). Phaedromus, talking about offerings to Venus (71–4) and making a libation of wine to summon Leaena (76–87), utters a prayer not to a god but to Cappadox' doors: "go on, drink, sacred doors, drink and become ready and favorable for me" (88–9). Once Leaena goes to fetch Planesium, Phaedromus makes a vow to her. A vow is the ritual promise of an offering to a divinity, in thanksgiving for a boon hoped to be granted by that deity. Phaedromus makes his with a jokey twist (140–40b):

> If you uphold your end of the bargain with me, I'll build you a wine-y statue rather than a gold one, to be a monument to your gullet.

Instead of the usual gold-standard offering—the sort that Therapontigonus would want for himself, according to Curculio (439–41)—Phaedromus figures he's found something more up Leaena's alcoholic alley. Phaedromus also sings a song to the bolts on Cappadox' door (147–55; Chapter 4). It is a ritual invocation, with flavors of both prayer and magical incantation. At the moment Planesium and Therapontigonus recognize one another as long-lost siblings, Phaedromus confers his blessing upon them: "I want the gods to make sure this turns out well for y'all" (658–9). Other than Cappadox himself, Phaedromus is the most religiously oriented character in the play.

Religion inflects the dialogue of Plautus' characters in less-overt ways, too. When Lyco makes a random guess that Curculio/"Summanus" lost his eye from a stray ember kicked up while cooking, Curculio notes in an aside, "this guy's a prophet, he predicts the future—'cause those're the kinds of catapults that launch at me most frequently" (397–8). The word I've translated as "prophet," *superstitiosus*, literally means, "full-of-awe-inspiring-wonder-as-if-caused-by-divine power." The religiously tinged idea in these lines matches something like "mindreader" in modern colloquial English. Along the same lines, Lyco and Therapontigonus use religious imagery in their fight later on in the play (537–9):

Lyco Goddamn, I'm not making you an offering of some run-of-the-mill misfortune, but the same stuff I usually offer somebody I don't owe nothing.

Therapontigonus Don't get all fierce with me and don't imagine I'm going to get on my knees and beg.

Lyco uses a word for religious offerings (*macto, mactare*) that has come to mean simply "to present," and Therapontigonus responds with a verb about begging (*supplicare*) that derives from a ritual of formally entreating a god or a mortal for help.

The best use of this sort of language in *Curculio*, I'd say, is how Curculio himself says he responded when the soldier invited him to dinner during his overseas trip. "It was a matter of religious scruples, I was unwilling to refuse" (350). As a gluttonous parasite, it is a question of piety and religious obligation for Curculio to take a free meal always and forever. This is a hilarious bit of playing around with Roman religious customs. It's a much less serious form of religious scruples, *religio*, than what Curculio's adversary Cappadox displays throughout the play.

A pious sex-trafficker?

The most religious character in *Curculio* is also the most reviled, the non-citizen sex-trafficker Cappadox. (Lyco the banker is similarly reviled yet pious, performing a *salutatio* of Aesculapius with head covered at 389–90.) Cappadox is unique among surviving instances of his stock type in Greek and Roman comedy, not only for his ritual activity but also for his comparatively substantial respect for laws, oaths, and Planesium. Sex-traffickers in other Plautine plays (*Persa*, *Poenulus*, *Pseudolus*, *Rudens*) are generally sacrilegious or blasphemous or indifferent to divine matters. Sex-traffickers in Plautus are likewise fraudulent and oathbreaking by default. But not Cappadox, who seems committed to the legal promises he has made (490–4) and expresses reluctance to commit perjury ("what about the fact that I swore an oath?," 458).

Before the sex-trafficker even appears on stage, Phaedromus mentions that he "is sick and doing an incubation ritual in the shrine of Aesculapius" (61–2), and spectators learn that the onstage altar belongs not to the shrine, but to Cappadox himself. In his first appearance, Cappadox indeed exits from the shrine, upset about receiving unfavorable omens from Aesculapius (216–18). He complains extensively about his illness (219–22). He then asks Palinurus for a *coniectura*, a dream-interpretation (245–50). After Palinurus passes him off to the Cook, he shares his dream (260–3), eagerly listens to the Cook's interpretation (270–2), and then, in accordance with the Cook's recommendation, heads off to offer renewed prayer to the god (273).

When Cappadox re-enters a couple hundred lines later, he makes no mention of his illness, and instead happily greets Lyco with a conventional, yet religiously tinged, hello ("may the gods love you,"

455). I think that Cappadox is feeling less sick by this point, and that the actor playing him may have changed costuming while back stage to appear less greenish and less bloated. Once Cappadox has transferred Planesium over to Phaedromus' house, the sex-trafficker heads back into the shrine to offer sacrifice: "since I've handled this business well, I want to make an offering in the shrine over here. . . . Now I'll turn my attention to sacrifice" (527 and 532).

Cappadox returns not much later with talk of successfully completing his sacrifice (557–8). When Therapontigonus and Curculio accost him at the end of the play, he calls upon the gods for protection (694) and invokes them in his curse of Phaedromus for not being an impartial arbiter (720). Cappadox talks religion in every scene he's in. He spends more time inside the shrine of Aesculapius than everywhere else combined, including on stage and in his own house. Out of his seven total entrances or exits in the whole play, five are motivated by religious observances.

What are we to make of this pious sex-trafficker? I see a direct connection between Cappadox' religiosity and his treatment of Planesium. When handing her over to Curculio, Cappadox says, "please take good care of her. I raised her well and in chastity at my house" (517–18). His expression of care for Planesium goes beyond a peddler making sure his merchandise is delivered intact. Planesium herself later echoes Cappadox verbatim (698), confirming the truth of his assertion. Therapontigonus' response to his sister's statement is dismissive (698–700):

> It's not like he [treated you kindly] *willingly*—you can thank Aesculapius here for your chastity, 'cause if that guy'd been healthier, he'd've long since sold you off wherever he could.

Of course, the person Cappadox would have sold her to is *the soldier himself*. The fact is that Cappadox didn't sell her to just anybody, and didn't put her into the brothel or the streets just as soon as he could. That's as it must be, since Planesium's chastity is an essential precondition for her to be eligible for marriage once she's been identified as a freeborn citizen.

The pious portrayal of Cappadox works in two directions at once. First, it humanizes him. Spectators see him doing something familiar from their own lives, something fundamental to their own societies and worldviews. This makes him less of a supervillain, more of a nuanced personality. At the same time, his religious activity makes things a little grimmer for the citizens in the crowd. They see him doing something familiar from their own lives, something fundamental to their own societies and worldviews. Cappadox is a nasty reminder that, in the Rome of Plautus, just as in his Epidaurus, some of the worst-dealing people are always to be found nearby, with more of a place in the physical and social and spiritual life of the City than the locals might like to admit.

The world that Plautus lived in shapes and is revealed by the world he creates on stage. Some of the most unsavory and gloomiest aspects of life in Rome pop up in *Curculio*, unexpectedly or otherwise. The traumas and horrors of enslavement, sex-labor, economic oppression, and poverty lurk behind this comedy of deception, desire, and family reunion. At the same time, as we examine the role of religion and ritual in the play, we uncover a portrait of a vibrant religious life day to day in the ancient Mediterranean, for the entire cross section of society, not just the elites.

It is my hope that over the past seven chapters you have gained a keen sense of what it might have been like to watch Plautus' *Curculio*: not only particulars of performance and wonders of the spectacle, hilarious action and ridiculous characters and clever plotting and subplotting, but also the experience of watching *Curculio* in Plautus' Rome, a wild and wooly and dirty and dreadful and exciting and upsetting City that—even if not truly Eternal—still claims a slice of immortality from its place in Plautine theater, a literary time capsule and time warp between two millennia ago and today. The last chapter will explore the time warp of Plautus' *Curculio* itself: how it survived from his day to ours, and how it has been reworked, revisited, and reimagined over the twenty-two centuries since it was written.

9

Curculio after Plautus

Well, dear reader, we're nearly at the end of our time together. For the past eight chapters we've been living in early second-century BCE Rome. In this chapter, we begin by hovering around the time of Plautus himself, to explore what the immediate afterlife of *Curculio* might have been after its first performance. Then we travel the timeline between Plautus' day and the advent of the printing press in Europe. Finally, we switch gears to observe how *Curculio* has been performed, adapted, and reimagined in the modern world, from the Renaissance to 2019.

How plays like *Curculio* were produced in the time of Plautus

The religious festivals at which Plautus' plays were performed were often organized by aediles, magistrates who had to arrange and pay for the events at their own expense. The aedile would be the one who hired Plautus to write a play, and the aedile would hire the acting troupe to perform it. The troupe might have been Plautus', in which case the aedile would just have to hire Plautus and he'd take care of the rest. Another important person was the choragus (Chapter 7), who had a collection of costumes and props available to lend to the troupe, and could probably be persuaded to purchase new ones when needed for a special purpose or a new play.

We can uncover a small economy of play production, all simply from the text of Plautus itself. It was a play, so it required actors, costumes, props, a stage. The stage wasn't permanent and so had to be constructed—

work for carpenters and painters. Props and costumes had to be made by somebody, too. Let's not forget the musical accompanist, the tibicen. Some or all of these laborers were enslaved, and the benefits of their labor and skill in this theatrical economy would accrue not to the people doing the labor but to the people who enslaved them.

Rome was likely where Plautus premiered his plays, but Rome wasn't Broadway: plays didn't happen all year 'round, even though festivals were pretty frequent. The actors would need to do something for work between big shows at Rome—and if the actors were enslaved, the troupe owner would want to be profiting off of them all year long. Meanwhile, Italy at the time of Plautus was full of nearby towns with Roman citizens and Italian allies who spoke Latin, the language of Plautus' plays. So, you should imagine that, after the premiere in Rome, the troupe would take the show on the road. A play like *Curculio* is a great traveling show. At each stop, the actor playing the Choragus could swap out the Roman references for local shout-outs. The troupe might plug its play into local festivals or might just set up shop and perform for as long as it seemed like people would pay.

Early receptions of *Curculio*

Evidence exists for the popularity of theater, both tragedy and comedy, across time and space in the ancient Mediterranean. What about *Curculio*? Was it a critical success and were people talking about it for weeks afterward? There's no way to know. No performance records survive, if any were ever even kept. No reviews by theater critics to tell us what elites thought, either. The best we can do for any of Plautus' plays is look for evidence of reperformance in the scripts themselves, and pay attention to references to Plautus in later authors. The prologue of Plautus' *Casina*, for example, makes clear that the text you can read today is from a revival of the play after Plautus' death. The later Roman author Cicero, meanwhile, claims (*De Senectute* 50) that Plautus himself in his old age most enjoyed *Truculentus* and *Pseudolus*; and Cicero's contemporary Varro, Plautus' biggest fan ever, alludes to situations from Plautus' *Amphitruo* and *Epidicus* in his satire "Bimarcus."

The most important early reception of Plautus' *Curculio* is another Roman comedy, Terence's *Phormio*, a generation after Plautus, and earlier than Cicero or Varro. The title character of Terence's play is, like Curculio, a parasite, and is, like Curculio, the play's star trickster. The prologue of *Phormio* explains, "the guy who'll play the central role is Phormio the parasite, who'll be mostly responsible for what happens" (27–8). This description of the play might prompt regular viewers of Roman comedy to think about *Curculio*.

Terence's *Phormio* echoes Plautus' *Curculio* on a couple different levels, from plot to character to specific theatrical moments. Young lover boy has fallen for a girl enslaved to a sex-trafficker, but doesn't have the cash to pay for her, and his father's not around, so the parasite comes up with a scheme to make it happen, while the enslaved attendant fails to play the trickster role. Am I describing the plot of *Curculio* or of *Phormio*? Both, actually. A key twist in Terence is that dad comes home partway through the play, complicating things further for Phormio. Phormio, like Curculio, ends up involved in some legal wrangling (*Phormio* 125–34). In *Phormio*, a man named Geta—like Palinurus in *Curculio*—is enslaved in the young lover boy's household, tries and fails to be the *callidus* (for instance, he needs Phormio's help to swindle cash from dad to purchase the beloved sex-laborer, 560), and is an ineffectual *paedagogus* (babysitter) for the young men in his care. Like Curculio himself, Geta willingly plays the role of enslaved errand-runner (*seruus currens*) to share bad news with the lover boy (177–230, reprised at 844–5).

When it comes to particular moments, the discussion in *Phormio* of how the young man can't secure a loan to pay for his girl (301–3) might remind us of a similar plot point in *Curculio* (329–34; or maybe a similar moment in Plautus' *Pseudolus* 80–6, 295–305). Elsewhere, when the lover boy is making an impassioned plea to the sex-trafficker, he says to him, "in my eyes, you're a relative, you're a parent, you're an ally, you're—" (497), at which point the sex-trafficker interrupts to shut him up. This sounds like it might be modeled on how Leaena in *Curculio* addresses her wine: "in my eyes, you're incense, you're cinnamon, you're roses, you're saffron and another-kind-of-cinnamon, you're fenugreek" (103–4). Finally, towards the end of *Phormio*, the title character falls into a scuffle with lover boy's dad, and when dad instructs his enslaved henchmen to attack Phormio, the parasite says, "why don't you carve out my eye?" (989). This is a very specific injury to invoke, and I think Terence is reminding us of Curculio's stint as the one-eyed Summanus (starting at 371). It's a metatheatrical wink (heh) at the Plautine model for Phormio and for *Phormio*.

From Terence we can move ahead to the time of Cicero and Varro, and look at the most famous poetry from the Late Republic, the countercultural erotic lyric and attack-poetry of Gaius Valerius Catullus (84–54 BCE). Christopher B. Polt argues that Catullus finds in Curculio, and in Plautine parasites more generally, a model for subverting elite Roman sensibilities about social norms. In the speech of the Choragus, meanwhile, it's possible to find keywords for Catullus' own poetic values: "charming" (*lepidus*), "trifles" (*nugae*), and wit (*sal*, or rather the Greek cognate *halophanta* in the Choragus' speech). But I think that the connection goes deeper, and our play specifically is influential in the creation of the witty, wily, misbehaved "Catullus" character of Catullus' poetry—because *Curculio*, uniquely of Plautus' surviving plays, gives us a clever character who is a citizen, unlike the more common enslaved tricksters or clever non-citizen sex-laborers.

How *Curculio* got from ancient Rome to your bookshelf

The actors who performed the plays of Plautus were most likely illiterate, and had to learn their lines and songs by ear, from Plautus himself or else someone involved in the production who could transmit Plautus' writing and musical composition to them. This tells us that the text of *Curculio* as we can read it today probably began life not as a rehearsal *script* for the actors but as some kind of a performance *transcript*, a record of how the play turned out. Additional evidence for this hypothesis comes from occasional spots in Plautine comedies where a joke is repeated or a routine of funny business goes on disproportionately long—signs of actors improvising material to add onto the play as Plautus wrote it, or extending in performance a bit that went over particularly well.

Plautus was popular enough in his own time that at least some Romans elite enough to be literate wanted copies of his comedies to read at their leisure. Terence probably had access to a text of *Curculio* when he was writing his own *Phormio*. Printing presses and publishing houses didn't exist in ancient Rome, and every text—literary or bureaucratic, important or forgettable, highbrow or vulgar—had to be written down by hand (often by enslaved scribes). Literate Plautus fans wanting to read *Curculio* might buy a copy, or instead borrow one from a friend and make a copy of it. We can talk about the works of Plautus (or of any other Greek or Roman author) being not *published* but *circulated*.

This is basically the story of the survival of *Curculio* in its first hundred or so years. People wanted to read it, so they would find copies of it and buy them or bootleg them. If *Curculio* hadn't been popular enough to stimulate such behavior, it wouldn't have had enough of a copying tradition to survive into the modern world.

The first Plautus director's cut

The first big milestone in the history of the text of *Curculio* is the Noah's Ark moment for Plautine comedy. A Roman named Marcus Terentius Varro Reatinus (116–27 BCE) was Plautus' biggest fanboy. Varro was a scholar, soldier, satirist, and statesman. He liked to figure out where things came from, especially words (etymology) and religious practices. His most important work of scholarship on Plautus was a critical assessment of which plays were truly Plautine and which weren't. By Varro's time, more than a hundred plays were circulating under the name "Plautus." He was such a popular comedian that any good comedy could plausibly be attributed to him, and any bad comedian could put their work out there by slapping Plautus' name on it. Varro took it upon himself to study the supposedly "Plautine" works out there and narrow them from the hundred-plus circulating under Plautus' name down to just the authentic ones.

What Varro actually wrote about this topic didn't make it into the modern world, but I can still tell you which plays he said were really Plautus' handiwork. They're the twenty-one (well, twenty-and-a-half) that have survived the process of copying, over and over again. And those twenty-one have survived because of Varro's judgment. He was "the most learned man in Rome" in his time according to the later Roman author Quintilian (*Institutio Oratoria* 10.1.95), and his collection of twenty-one plays, the ones he and everyone he consulted said for sure were authentically Plautine, became the definitive collection in Roman culture. The rest were eventually discarded and lost to the metaphorical Flood of passing centuries.

The manuscript tradition

Varro's selection of Plautus was copied—and thus *Curculio* was copied—by Romans and their enslaved scribes again and again throughout the centuries of Roman dominance in the Mediterranean world. When later authors refer or allude to Plautus, that means they're reading him, or maybe even seeing revival performances. Varro's contemporary Cicero specifically discusses actors playing parts in Plautine plays, and another contemporary, Catullus, fills his poetry with characters and scenarios that sound like they're straight from Plautus. In the generation after Varro, the poet Horace (65–8 BCE) mentions both Plautus and Terence. On and on, through the Roman Empire's rise, reign, and fall. There's even a fourth-century CE comedy, *Querolus*, that adapts a play of Plautus, with Christian elements added in.

Plautus doesn't disappear in the Middle Ages, but his influence and popularity are on the wane. While his texts haven't disappeared, they have become fewer and farther between. The manner of transmission of Latin literary texts during the Middle Ages is much the same. Scribes—mostly Catholic monks, working in monasteries—laboriously copy each text word for word by hand. (Arabic scholars in mediaeval Baghdad and elsewhere did the same with many translations of classical texts, especially Greek philosophy, medicine, and science.) This process of textual transmission across the ages is called the manuscript tradition. But a lot of the conditions of copying have changed between Rome and the mediaeval monks. Monks live austere lives, so you should probably imagine them making copies while sitting on a hard bench in uncomfortable clothes in an unheated, poorly lit room during the cold midwinter, with little in the way of hearty food and no caffeine to ease their toils. In fact, the monks copying these manuscripts occasionally scribbled complaints in the margin: about illness, hangovers, crummy writing utensils, and the shoddy work of their peers.

Medieval monks knew Latin, to be sure, but the Latin of the Romans was not the monks' native language, and the Latin of Plautus is, even for Roman-era Latin, archaic, colloquial, and simply wild. So, sackcloth copyists would have had difficulty understanding what they were reading, and Plautus' music and meter would have been totally beyond most of them. Plautus' comedies, with their overt sexuality and polytheism, crossed several moral and religious boundaries for the poor monks.

Bad working conditions, inadequate Latin skills, and divergent worldviews took their toll on the text of Plautus during this period. Unlike the Roman poet Vergil, whose epic *Aeneid* survives in dozens of copies from as early as the fourth century, only one copy of Plautus survives from within a thousand years of Plautus' own time. That one (from the fifth century CE) and the next-oldest-surviving copies are all plagued with many problems: spelling errors, missing chunks, messed-up line breaks, additions that aren't authentically Plautine (bogus bonus material), garbled passages, and even literal holes in the paper. One play, Plautus' *Vidularia*, was unlucky enough to be last alphabetically in Varro's collection, and most of it was lost somewhere along the way, never to be read again.

Curculio does not survive intact in the oldest, fifth-century manuscript of Plautus, which was held in an abbey in northern Italy and did not resurface until 1815. Of the three next-oldest manuscripts, all from the mediaeval period, *Curculio* is contained in only one, from the tenth century. But from that manuscript, a number of copies that include the text of *Curculio* survive, among them one from eleventh-century Italy, two from eleventh-century France, another from twelfth-century Italy, and one from twelfth-century England. How thin the thread from which our play dangles.

From manuscript to modern translation

Once Europeans figured out how to do something that Chinese inventors had introduced centuries earlier—the printing press with moveable type—the biography of the text of *Curculio* changed dramatically. It wasn't necessary any more to spend long, long hours writing out a copy of the text by hand, with lots of opportunities for mistakes along the way. The *editio princeps* is the first printed—rather than handwritten—version of Plautus' plays. The *editio princeps* of Plautus was produced by Giorgio Merula in Venice in 1472; printings of Plautus' first eight plays alphabetically, including *Curculio*, seem to have been made before Merula's edition, but none of those have survived. Escaping manuscripts and entering print kickstarted Plautus' popularity both among fans of Roman literature and, more importantly, as a model for authors of comedy in the fifteenth to twentieth centuries.

By this point, the centuries and centuries of hand copyists had done their damage to Varro's collection of Plautine comedy. Printing the words that appeared in a manuscript wasn't enough to get close to the text as Plautus might actually have written it. It entails reflecting on all potential sources of error in order to realize that the manuscript tradition alone is insufficient. But eventually scholars started working on critical editions of Greek and Latin texts, including Plautus. Putting together a critical edition of a text requires looking at as many manuscripts of that text as possible, especially the earliest manuscripts that still survive. You compare their readings—what they have for each given word or phrase or line—and try to determine which reading is best, which reading is most likely to be what the author originally wrote. You may also make conjectures to replace readings that you think the manuscripts have messed up, based on your knowledge of Latin, of the author's style, and of the sorts of errors that copyists tended to make over the centuries. You might even try to fill in gaps in the text where the manuscript tradition has lost something.

A lot of subjective thinking is involved in doing a critical edition, so one person's critical edition is never enough. The first critical edition of Plautus came 80 years after the *editio princeps*. It was produced in 1552 by Joachim Camerarius in Basel, Switzerland. In the 468 years between when that came out and when I'm writing this, many scholars, have pored over the manuscripts and the texts, the conjectures of earlier scholars and the most cutting-edge criticism of Plautus' style, in order to try to approximate better what Plautus actually wrote. The most recent critical edition of *Curculio*, quoted throughout this book, was published in 2008 in Italy, the work of Settimio Lanciotti, part of a multi-decade undertaking by the University of Urbino to produce new critical editions of each of Plautus' plays, which as a whole haven't had a new one since the early 1900s.

But not everybody knows Latin. Scholars who wanted to bring Plautus to a wider readership translated his works into vernacular languages, the languages people actually spoke and read. Since Plautus' language and themes are so down to earth and colloquial, it's hard to evaluate translations of him from times distant from our own, so I won't undertake an exhaustive translation history. Suffice it to say that *Curculio* isn't the most-frequently translated play by Plautus, and tends to be translated anew only when someone's doing a complete set of all 21 surviving Plautine works. As a result, while the first translation of a play by Plautus (his *Menaechmi*) into English appeared in 1595, no complete English translation of Plautus, including *Curculio*, was produced until the 1700s.

The 2006 translation of *Curculio* by Amy Richlin is the most adventuresome translation of *Curculio* I know of in any language. Her approach to translation emphasizes the immediacy and fleetingness of the experience of Plautine humor: jokes that land right away, without explanation, but jokes that keep on coming and don't wait for you, don't last beyond the day, and often won't age well. Richlin also focuses on how Plautus shows us the anxieties, oppressions, wartime mindset, and prejudices of his audience, with its diverse cross section of Roman society. One illustration of this approach is her translation of the long list of peoples that Curculio (as "Summanus") says Therapontigonus has been conquering (442–6): Persians, Paphlagonians, Cretans, and so forth become "the Iranians, the Kurds, Tehranians, Arabs, Palestinians, Jordanians," and so on. Richlin seeks to translate not just at the level of words, but at the level of *cultures*—so she translates real, actual places that Roman imperialism was sending Roman soldiers in Plautus' time with real, actual places that American imperialism has sent American soldiers and covert operatives in our own era. Similarly, she puts her Choragus not into the Roman Forum, but in New York City, whose landmarks are as familiar to American readers as the Forum's were to Roman viewers, even if they're spread across Manhattan rather than concentrated within the same small part of Rome's downtown.

How *Curculio* has been adapted and performed in the modern world

Curculio on the modern stage has a history that stretches back to the late 1400s. We begin with *Curculio* as first performed after Roman times. Several works from the last five hundred years adapt or reimagine or allude to or build on Plautus' *Curculio*. Finally, I will consider performances of *Curculio* from 1490 to 2019. (The initial draft of that sentence ended with "2020," but the COVID-19 pandemic cancelled a performance of *Curculio* by my students at Wake Forest University scheduled for April of that year.)

The earliest recorded performances of *Curculio*

The first performance of *Curculio* isn't documented. Neither are any others that may have taken place in the ancient Roman world. We have to jump 1,700 years to find the first one that is. In 1479, a humanist in Verona by the name of Guarino or Guarini translated Plautus' *Curculio* and *Aulularia* into Italian and sent it to Ercole I d'Este, Duke of Ferrara. Both plays were performed in Ferrara in 1490 and 1503. The translations are lost, so it's nearly impossible to say anything about the performances, other than that the translator described his translation approach to the Duke as "I force myself to follow the words of the text," which I take to mean that he aimed for a close, literal translation, even if it meant the jokes weren't quite as funny as they could have been, or the dialogue didn't sound quite as colloquial as it would have to Plautus' audiences.

The next performance of *Curculio* on record is in 1563, at Jesus College, Cambridge University, performed in Latin. This was during the reign of Elizabeth, and, in fact, she saw a performance of another Plautine play, *Aulularia*, during her visit to Cambridge in 1564. Cambridge University and its rival Oxford University have a long tradition of performing Greek and Roman plays in their original languages, and *Curculio* is one of the earliest plays performed at Jesus College specifically, only two years after the college began staging ancient plays. It's the first known performance of *Curculio* on a college campus, a popular site for revivals of the play. After the 1563 performance, the next one of *Curculio* I could find reference to was in 1981. Performances that occurred in the meantime have been lost to history.

Literary reboots of *Curculio*

Even if the recorded early performances of *Curculio* are few and far between, plenty of evidence exists for the influence of the play in another arena: plays that adapt or allude to or draw on Plautus' comedy. A good example is the Italian Renaissance-era *commedia dell'arte*, a semi-improvisational routine-based comedy with stock characters and stock plots heavily indebted to Roman comedy. One such stock character, Ligurio, is, like Curculio himself, a parasite and a trickster, on par with Plautus' greatest *serui callidi*.

But perhaps the earliest reworking of *Curculio* in the modern world is, surprisingly, the work of the man who would become Pope Pius II (reigned 1458–64), Enea Silvio Bartolomeo Piccolomini. Fourteen years before ascending to the papacy, Piccolomini wrote a comedy in Latin, *Chrysis* ("Goldie"), one of the few works from his pre-pope life he didn't burn. In it, he draws heavily on Plautus, imitating or even directly copying lines or whole passages at once. Piccolomini uses *Curculio* in particular for the winetastic cameo by Leaena, ported into his play for the drunken old woman Canthara, whose name refers to a large ancient Greek drinking vessel. Similar imitations and borrowings crop up in *Annularia* ("The Play about the Ring") and *Bophilaria* ("The Play about the Cowherd"), two Latin comedies published in 1505 by Egidio Gallo, an Italian humanist from Rome.

Similarly, *A Very Woman, or The Prince of Tarent*, an English tragicomedy written by Philip Massinger and John Fletcher (published 1655, probably written between 1619 and 1622) has a scene involving a trail of spilled wine meant to draw out a guardian named Borachia (her name possibly a reference to "borracha," a Spanish word for "drunk woman"?), and all of Borachia's scenes may be modeled on *Curculio*. Ben Jonson, in his 1610 English play *The Alchemist*, alludes to something Palinurus says about Leaena. Then, as a wink and a nod to anybody who caught his *Curculio* reference, Jonson punningly hints at the play's title by writing in the words "corns" and "worm," because another word for curculio is "corn-worm."

For Stephen Gosson, an anti-theater activist in sixteenth-century England, *Curculio* functions as a sign of how smart he is: in *Schoole of Abuse* (1579), he name-drops our parasite in a passage about how plays in his own time would filter Plautus to be inoffensive to contemporary sensibilities. Likewise, while praising the food of England's inns, even in poor villages, Fynes Moryson's 1617 *An Itinerary* remarks, "if Curculio of Plautus should see the thatched houses he would fall into a fainting of his spirits, but if he should smell the variety of meats his starveling look would be much cheered." In George Chapman's 1602 English comedy *The Gentleman Usher*, a character named Sarpego says he once played the part of Curculio in a performance in Italy—and then he goes on to put on a costume and do Curculio's opening lines in Latin!

For the French playwright Molière, *Curculio* supplies a major theatrical plot point. Molière's *L'Étourdi ou les Contretemps* ("The Blunderer, or the Counterplots," 1655) is a comedy generically in the style of Plautus, with different tricksters interfering with each other's schemes. The ultimate resolution is very specific to *Curculio*, because it depends on one rival for the beloved turning out to be her long-lost brother instead. (Molière's play was directly modeled on Niccolò Barbieri's 1629 play *L'Innavertito*, "The Careless Guy," and then was itself the model for Dryden's hugely successful 1667 play *Sir Martin Mar-all.*) About a century earlier, Giovanni Maria Cecchi's *I rivali* ("The Rivals," uncertain date; Cecchi lived from 1518 to 1587) borrowed the Cappadox/Planesium/Phaedromus storyline from *Curculio*, shifting the sex-trafficker to a low-status innkeeper, and making the young man's goal marriage all along. In 1772, the German playwright Jakob Michael Reinhold Lenz wrote an entire play modeled on *Curculio*, which he titled *Die Türkensklavin*, "The Enslaved Woman from Turkey." His approach is to focus on the comic action and plotline, while cutting out Plautus' signature banter, metatheatrically self-aware characters, and clash of styles and statuses.

Jump ahead 200 years and we find the Dutch illustrator Magda van Tilburg's graphic novel of *Curculio*, originally published in 1980 and republished digitally in color in 2008. The 2008 version, vibrantly garish, features Latin dialogue with English translation in the margin. The Choragus scene is cut out, but otherwise the action of every scene is faithfully represented, while dialogue is abridged and condensed; most of the jokes are gone, as are some key bits of plot-related information. Planesium gives off vixen-like, femme-fatale vibes. Lyco, Cappadox, and Curculio convey fear of Therapontigonus in their arguments with him, unlike in Plautus. The quality of the whole graphic novel is marred by the intensely anti-Semitic depiction of Lyco the greedy banker—not a young man as in Plautus, but an old, somewhat effeminate, balding man with an unrealistically large nose.

Plautus goes to Broadway, then Hollywood

The biggest moment for *Curculio* in the twentieth century was *A Funny Thing Happened on the Way to the Forum*, a musical by Burt Shevelove, Larry Gelbart, and Stephen Sondheim that premiered on Broadway in 1962 and was made into a feature film in 1966. *Funny Thing* is a Plautus mashup, with a lot of the familiar stock types (Pseudolus the enslaved trickster from Plautus' *Pseudolus*; Miles Gloriosus the blowhard soldier, after Plautus' *Miles Gloriosus*) and a blend of stock plots from a few plays, including *Curculio*. In the program for the 2004 production by the National Theatre, Sondheim (who wrote the songs) says that Shevelove gave him the Loeb Classical Library translations of Plautus, which include *Curculio*, to read when they were preparing the musical. Gelbart's introduction to the 1991 publication of the script of *Funny Thing* doesn't mention *Curculio*, but it only mentions two plays of Plautus, leaving out plays that were unquestionably influential on the writing of the Broadway show.

The basic plot of *Funny Thing* is this: lover boy wants enslaved sex-laborer (miraculously a virgin) from next door, but doesn't have the cash, and meanwhile a soldier is on his way to pick her up. Deception plots and hijinx ensue. Thanks to signet rings—the recognition tokens—soldier turns out to be enslaved sex-laborer's long-lost brother. (The movie version also adds in a chariot chase scene, in a nod to the sword-and-sandal film genre so popular in the 1950s and 1960s.) Plenty comes from other Plautine plays, including a supposedly haunted house from *Mostellaria*, a horny old dad and cross-gender-disguise subplot from *Casina*, and those title characters from *Pseudolus* and *Miles Gloriosus*. But, as with Molière, the recognition scene at the end is specifically, pointedly *Curculio*—as is the fact that *Funny Thing* keeps quiet about near-miss incest between sister sex-laborer and brother soldier. With

Curculio in mind, you might even take the musical's title, *A Funny Thing Happened on the Way to the Forum*, as a description of the monologue of the Choragus.

Funny Thing was an instant hit, and has been an enduring favorite for fans of musicals over the past sixty years. It's been done and redone all across the globe, translated into other languages, and is a solid choice for student and professional productions. At the time it was produced, it was a piece of countercultural resistance. It fused Plautus' theater of the lower classes with actors and writers from marginalized groups in the mid-century United States. It featured Jewish-American actors and starred Zero Mostel, who had been blacklisted during the Red Scare in the 1950s. It has loads of camp: a self-aware, over-the-top style of acting that plays with social norms about sexuality and gender expression. For the director of the film version, Richard Lester, *Funny Thing* aimed to push against Hollywood tropes and stereotypes by showing the dark side of ancient Rome, with particular attention to enslavement and oppression (although the movie itself is guilty of exoticized, sexual depictions of two enslaved sex-laborers of color). Here, too, I think it draws on *Curculio*, which sheds similar light on oppressive conditions in Plautus' Rome.

Curculio on college campuses

Curculio has turned out to be quite popular to perform on college campuses over the past few decades. In 1981, a performance was put on at Wellesley College (in Wellesley, Massachusetts) by students of the Departments of Greek and Latin. It was performed in Latin, and the program included lists of "words to listen for," a guide to Latin-learners and -enthusiasts as they watched the performance. The program's cover featured rings, in a nod to the play's most important props: one was labeled, in Latin, "the ring of Curculio the parasite," the other "the ring of Therapontigonus the soldier." Therapontigonus' ring had a big sword and an elephant split in half, as described in Plautus' script (424), plus the Latin legend "I fight, therefore I am," while Curculio's ring had a depiction of dice and the mottos, "don't be tricked, do the tricking" and "I'm hungry, therefore I am." A decade later, the Rugby School (Rugby, England) put on its own Latin production of *Curculio*, in mid-June, 1991. This was early in a series of annual Rugby performances of Plautus plays in Latin under the direction of Keith Maclennan, with a focus on staying close to the Latin text but updating the costumes to a roughly 1930s aesthetic.

Most recently, in April 2019, some of my own students at Wake Forest University put on a 9-minute, heavily adapted version of *Curculio* that intentionally drew out some of the awkwardness of the near-miss incest between Planesium and Therapontigonus, rather than sweeping it under the rug like *Funny Thing* did. Meanwhile, 2018 saw a full-scale production of *Curculio*, translated into Czech, at Masaryk University in Brno, Czech Republic. This performance is notable for its introduction of a new character, Footnote, an outside-the-story, fourth-wall-breaking figure, who patiently and humorously explains (Figure 9.1) historical context, untranslatable puns, stock characters, and plot details. She sometimes argues with characters inside the story, or actors peeking their heads out from backstage, too. The Czech production was reprised in October 2019.

The most play *Curculio* has had in the last hundred years is at the Virginia Governor's Latin Academy, a three-week intensive summer program held each year for the state's top 45 high-school Latin students, on a college campus somewhere in the state. The Academy did a performance specifically of *Curculio* every year from 1992 through 1999, with reprises in 2005 and 2011–13; at least six different directors have helmed the productions over the years. The performances were in Latin, working from the same script each year (Allan G. Gillingham's 1968 abridgement *Plautus for Reading and Production*, which cuts out the Choragus entirely). Minor changes reflected occasional cross-gender casting (e.g., Palinura instead of Palinurus when played by a woman), and cuts to bring the runtime down to 45 minutes, plus reduce the number of lines to memorize. Plenty of bit parts and extras, too, to accommodate students who didn't want to act but did want to wear a

Figure 9.1 "Footnote" breaking the fourth wall in the October 2019 Czech production of *Curculio aneb Darmojed*. Photo by Marek Augustin, retrieved from http://classics.phil.muni.cz/Plautus.

costume and run around (or, in at least one case, tap-dance, and in at least one other, play the tuba). Starting in 1996, most roles were given masks and split between two actors, because the performers, not being trained actors, found memorizing their lines too taxing.

The best-documented performances of *Curculio* have been productions at St. Olaf College (Northfield, Minnesota). Almost every year since 1982, the Classics department at St. Olaf has put on a play by Plautus; in 1995, 2005, and 2016, the play was *Curculio*, under the direction of Anne H. Groton. The target audiences are middle and high school Latin students, as well as some colleges. As a result, the adaptations are extensive, removing sexual content and alcohol references—but often retaining enslavement, as fits our twisted American sensibilities—and inserting more-relatable jokes and character types. The plays are performed mostly in English, though some Latin is included, usually with an English translation right after; over time, the scripts have tended to become shorter, with less Latin.

Music comes in the form of ditties written by Groton herself, sometimes varying between English and Latin verses, often with the audience invited to sing along to the chorus. In 2005, the cast was large, so the Cook role was played by four people, with four "apprentices" added, and Cappadox was given an entourage of four singing nurses. The 2016 production superimposed an animal theme (specifically, cats and dogs) onto the play, in order to hold the attention of the youngest members of the audience.

Finally, for my money, the most influential production of *Curculio* in the last century took place at Trent University (in Peterborough, Canada) in March 1996, under the direction of C. W. Marshall. Working from a new translation of the play by Peter L. Smith, Marshall attempted to replicate as best as possible the original performance conditions of the play, with an impromptu stage outdoors in a heavily trafficked area on campus. Actors wore masks and improvised, and all roles were played by just six actors. All characters were represented by half-masks in the style of renaissance Italian *commedia dell'arte*, and only Curculio had a full-face mask, with a long, phallic, proboscis-like nose. Leaena's entry song was set to the tune of Strauss' *Blue Danube*, and each character was distinguished not only by their mask but also by distinctive, recurrent gestures. As for why I rate this production so important: Marshall tells me that producing *Curculio* is what prompted him to write his book, *The Stagecraft and Performance of Roman Comedy*—one of the most important books about Plautus (and Terence) in a generation.

Why *Curculio*?

The obvious answer to the question is that it's short. It's manageable, not too many lines to memorize, won't test your audience's patience. A utilitarian answer, to be sure. But remember that utilitarian things can be, you know, *useful*, and so our play rises to the top when directors are looking for a quick-and-dirty splash in the Plautine pond. That's not the whole story, though.

Interestingly to me, the answer does *not* seem to include the speech of the Choragus—something that we've seen is fascinating in and of itself and also perfect for adaptation. Many of the productions I've surveyed simply cut the monologue and the character out, or replace them with an unrelated song. For instance, a 2014 Spanish-language youth community theater production of *Curculio* (produced by the Asociación cultural Taetro in Chiclana de la Frontera, Spain; Eufrasio Jiménez Verdugo and Miguel Ángel Bolaños, directors) cut out the Choragus scene to make room for a new character: the god Cupid, who gave an introductory prologue previewing the erotic plot of the play about to be performed, and delivered a wrap-up monologue added on after Plautus' final line. A notable exception is a 2016 student production at Brigham Young University (BYU), Provo, Utah, newly translated and directed by Seth Jeppesen, in which the Choragus shows up as a nervous backstage techie who stalls for time by reading her poem, a series of rhymes about where you can find students with different majors on BYU's campus. Marshall's 1996 Trent University production similarly adapted the Choragus' lines to the campus setting, while the 1981 Wellesley performance seems to have retained the Choragus' monologue unchanged.

Curculio, like other plays by Plautus, is a common choice for performances of plays, in Latin or English or a hybrid, aimed at Latin-student audiences. This is the case for some of the campus productions we've just encountered, such as St. Olaf's; for a 1962 production of *Curculio* in adapted Latin at Phillips Academy in Andover, Massachusetts; and a 1998 production by Theater Ludicrum at the Strand Theater in Dorchester, Massachusetts (newly translated and directed by George Bisanstrin, original music by Matthew Wulff, with special showings for Latin students). On the one hand, we could say these didactic productions of Plautus just boil down to cultural tourism, a fun but shallow and short-term visit to a foreign place whose worst problems are swept under the rug for our benefit as viewers and voyeurs. Not just metaphorical tourism, but actual tourism, too: *Curculio* has been performed (Giancarlo Sammartano, director) in the archaeological sites of ancient Graeco-Roman theaters and amphitheaters at Fiesole in Italy, Syracuse in Sicily, Carnuntum in Austria, and Mérida in Spain (all in 1991), and at Segesta and Morgantina, again in Sicily (1993, with music composed by Stefano Marcucci). On the other hand, *Curculio*—with its full cast of stock characters and mashup of typical plotlines—can be a great introduction to the complexities of Plautine comedy, Roman humor, and Roman society, as I think this book has shown.

Call me biased, but I think it's high time for a full-fledged, professional production of *Curculio*. Sure, it's captured some very niche audiences, but it deserves to break into the theater world more broadly. *Curculio* is a tightly constructed tour de force of comedy. Its showcasing of the underbelly of Roman society practically begs its audiences to examine their own. And its Choragus prompts us to think about place, space, and the interactions between the world of comedy and the world of real life in a way that few plays can manage to do.

Conclusion: A round of applause for *Curculio*

Curculio sure does have a lot to say for itself, for such a short play. It draws us immediately into the action with a curious nighttime procession, and keeps up a fast pace of action and jokes as it runs through three classic Plautine plots. Along the way, it showcases Plautus' unrivaled musical technique, demonstrates just how much theater depends on props, messes around with metatheater and the boundaries between fiction and reality, and takes a deep dive into the ugly side of life in Epidaurus and Rome. *Curculio* does it all in 729 lines of the most rambunctious Latin you can find.

I'd like to end on a note of wonder. When you grasp a copy of *Curculio* in your hands, you're holding onto a time capsule of funny business that made people laugh more than twenty centuries ago. If you read it like I do, then you know it can still make people laugh today. (As my mom said to me when we were going over edits of Chapter 2, "It just feels so *current*!") *Curculio* is a connection through time and space, a link across the ages between cultures that are very foreign to one another—after all, what would Plautus have to say about NASCAR or cat memes?—but that still share some common ground for what tickles our funny bones. *Curculio* is a time traveler, journeying two millennia through untold perils and countless hands to make us chuckle. And I expect *Curculio* will, if climate chaos doesn't first turn our planet to ash, still be at it two millennia from now.

Key Terms and Definitions

alliteration A stylistic device involving repetition of consonants, especially at beginnings of words.

blocking Stuff that happens during a play that isn't dialogue or scenery: actions that actors take, from movement to gesture to use of props to facial expressions.

blocking character An antagonist: someone who prevents the play's main character from accomplishing their goals.

breaking the fourth wall When a character in a play or TV show or movie acknowledges the existence of the audience, and thus metatheatrically shatters the spectators' illusion that they are eavesdropping unnoticed.

cantica Rhythmically elaborate songs (showstoppers) in comedies of Plautus.

choragus A person contracted to provide costumes (and possibly build the stage) for theatrical performances; in *Curculio*, a surprising and showstopping onstage character.

elision In Latin poetry, elimination of the final syllable of a word; it happens when the word ends in a vowel (or vowel + M) and the following word begins with a vowel (or H + vowel). Sort of like contractions in English (don't, wouldn't, I'd've, wanna, imma).

fabulae palliatae The subgenre of Roman comedy that Plautus writes.

fourth wall *See* breaking the fourth wall.

Greek New Comedy The genre of theater that Plautus translates and adapts.

iambic senarius The second most common pattern of poetic line rhythms in Plautus; the only line rhythm that was spoken, without accompaniment by the tibicen.

labeling function of props When props are used to denote a character (e.g., a sword for a soldier) or other aspect of a play (e.g., a candle to show it's nighttime).

libation A religious ritual in ancient Greece and Rome that involved pouring wine out onto the ground (or atop an altar) in honor of a deity.

mechanical function of props When props are used to advance the plot of a play forward, such as when a signet ring is used to forge documents or certify the identity of a long-lost sibling.

Menander The chief surviving author of Greek New Comedy, and one of a number of authors whose plays were adapted by both Plautus and Terence.

meretrix The Latin word for sex-laborer, and a stock type in Roman comedy.

metatheater When theater talks about theater, or acknowledges that it is theater, or there's a play within a play.

parasite A stock character in ancient comedy: glutton, mooch, hanger-on, brown-noser. Resorts to whatever flattery, trickery, witticisms, or self-debasement is required for a free meal.

paratragedy Parody of tragedy.

Plautus The reason you're reading this book. THM's favorite comedian.

seruus callidus A stock character in Plautus' comedy: an enslaved trickster, often star of the show.

sex-laborer (1) A free person who has sex for money, whether by choice (a "sex-worker") or, as in the ancient Greek and Roman worlds, because of coercive economic conditions. (2) An enslaved person forced to have sex for the profit of the person enslaving them.

stock character A stereotype or archetype, a familiar personality with a set of expectations that individual instantiations of the character will depart from or play around with, like the jock or nerd in high-school TV shows, or the *seruus callidus* or parasite in Roman comedy.

stock plot A stereotypical, routine plot that some works of literature use as a basis for creative storytelling, with individual twists and innovations.

symbolic function of props When props are used to symbolize something about a character or play, such as when a soldier's extremely oversized (or undersized) sword indicates his self-importance (or impotence).

Terence Publius Terentius Afer (195–159 BCE, maybe?), the second major surviving playwright of Roman Comedy after Plautus.

tibicen The accompanist in Roman comedy, who played the tibiae, a pair of double-reed woodwind pipes.

tricolon A stylistic device consisting of a series of three words or phrases, often increasing in length from first to third.

trochaic septenarius The most common pattern of poetic line rhythms in Plautus; sung to the accompaniment of the tibicen.

Notes and Recommended Reading

For the Latin text of Plautus' *Curculio*, I use the edition of Lanciotti (2008). All translations are my own. There isn't a fantastic English translation of *Curculio* out there, but the translation of de Melo (2011) is a mostly reliable guide to what the Latin actually says, and Richlin (2006) provides a slangy rendering with a focus on how the play communicates Roman racial prejudices about peoples to the east of Italy. Wright (1993) offers a Latin text with a commentary in English aimed at intermediate Latin students, while Gellar-Goad (forthcoming d) is a comprehensive commentary.

Chapter 1

For a start on the topic of ancient Greeks and Romans not being white, see Bond (2017) and McCoskey (2012). For an evocative description of the messiness of daily life in Rome, see Wiseman (1985: 1–14). Shelton (1997) furnishes an excellent compilation of ancient sources on Roman daily life.

A great general reference for the ancient Greek and Roman worlds is Hornblower, Spawnforth, and Eidinow (2012); I have referred to it here and there in my description of Roman festivals in this chapter. The idea that Curculio enters through the crowd belongs to Marshall (2006: 76).

Exactly who the audience was of Plautus' plays has been the subject of significant debate among scholars of Roman comedy. I side with Richlin (2017), who argues for an inclusive cross section of society, with plenty of material written specifically for enslaved and low-status spectators.

For an overview of any aspect of Latin literature that's more detailed than what I give here for Plautus, consult Conte (1999). For an introduction to Roman drama, read Moore (2012b); for a deeper dive into the details of Roman comedy, Duckworth (1952). The most important work on what makes Plautus' adaptations distinct from his Greek originals is Fraenkel (2007), whose title, *Plautine Elements in Plautus*, I allude to in this chapter.

"Dick Bozo Tapdancer": Damen (2012). Pieczonka (2019) discusses connections between the Plautine parasite and the Dossennus of Atellan farce. Plautine comedy's "Saturnalian spirit": Segal (1968).

I take the observation about *Curculio* having almost every stock type from von Antonsen-Resch (2005: 82). *Curculio* as a Plautus original: Lefèvre (1991). The possibility that Plautus has eliminated scenes from his Greek original: Fantham (1965).

Chapter 2

I discuss the "love" plot in *Curculio* also at Gellar-Goad (forthcoming a), in Italian. On Plautus and the marriage plot, see James (2020). An iMessage chat with Patrick J. Dombrowski gave helpful insight on my point about the "witness"/"testicle" pun at *Curculio* 31. On "Pick-Up Artists" and their misuses of Roman literature for misogynistic purposes, see Zuckerberg (2018: 89–142). My thinking on near-miss incest between Planesium and Therapontigonus was shaped by Witzke (2015b) and Slater (2001). On Plautus, war, and Roman imperialism, see Leigh (2004) and Burton (2020).

Chapter 3

The animal theme is laid out in brief by Wiles (1991: 137). For the identification of the scent at 101, I rely on Gitner (2016). Studies of banking in *Curculio* have been undertaken by Andreau (1968) and André (1983), both in French, and Giangreco Passi (1981), in Italian. Scafuro (1997: 175–80, 429–33, 442–3, 457–8) discusses law in *Curculio* (in English!). *Stuprum* can be committed against married or unmarried women or against citizen youths of any gender: see Fantham (1991). The theme of illness is detailed by Philippides (2018). For the urinary etymology of Palinurus, see Papaioannou (2008/2009).

Chapter 4

The definitive work on music and dance in Roman comedy is Moore (2012a), along with Marshall (2006: 203–44); much of my discussion here relies on these two sources. For a user-friendly introduction to music and meter in Plautus, read Gellar-Goad (2020); for a guide to Moore's work on music in Roman comedy, see Gellar-Goad (2014). For anything having to do with the rhythms of the cantica of Plautus, consult Questa (1995). On music in *Curculio* specifically, there's Ludwig (1967), if you can read German, and Augello (1983) and Moore (2005), if you can read Italian, plus a couple of tidbits (in English) in Moore (1998a: 245, 258–9). To learn how to recite trochaic septenarii without a lot of hassle, consult Moore (2012–13).

I take the "arc" concept from Marshall (2006: 207–8). All of my statistics on the frequency of metrical types in Plautus, and descriptions of the theatrical effects of the different meters, derive from Moore (2012a). For the scansion of the canticum, I rely on Questa (1995). The mock-solemnity of bacchiacs and cretics in *Curculio* is noted by Moore (2005: 20–1). Ketterer (1986: 196) makes the observation that Phaedromus' hymn is the earliest Roman example of the paraclausithyron. The structural role of the door in this scene's music is discussed by Moore (2005: 22).

I learned about the allusion to Sappho at *Curculio* 178–80 from Radif (2005). My discussion of dance in *Curculio* is indebted to Moore (2012a: 105–34). Habinek (2005: 116–17) argues for *Curculio* 295 being about a dance battle, while Richlin (2017: 158 n. 29, 206, 206 n. 3) takes it as a sexual reference. The observation that *ludii* at 150 can mean both "dancer" and "actor" is made by Moore (2012a: 106).

Chapter 5

The best discussion of the stagecraft and performance of Roman comedy is Marshall (2006), aptly titled *The Stagecraft and Performance of Roman Comedy*. I learned much of what I know on this topic from scholars and participants in the 2012 National Endowment for the Humanities institute, "The Performance of Roman Comedy," Chapel Hill, North Carolina, directed by Sharon L. James and Timothy J. Moore.

Cohen (2007) has experimented with mask-making techniques that would have been possible in ancient Rome and that result in masks with loudness-increasing effects. The rest of my discussion of costumes and masks depends largely on Marshall (2006: 56–66, 126–58). Animalistic masks for *Curculio* is the suggestion of Wiles (1991: 137). On racism and Roman attitudes towards Greeks, see McCoskey (2012: 39, 73–4, 119, 153–4). The lightning-fast eyepatch disguise of Curculio is noted by Marshall (2006: 60). The term "Plautinopolis" was coined by Gratwick (1982: 104).

Ketterer (1986) offers a groundbreaking analysis of props in *Curculio*; from there, I have borrowed the terms "labeling," "mechanical," and "symbolic," as well as a number of this chapter's particular observations on props in *Curculio*. The play's "circuits of exchange" also comes from Ketterer (ibid.: 204). Sharrock (2008) uses props as a launching-point for meditation on the materiality of things in *Curculio*.

It's been debated whether Therapontigonus leaves the stage at 590 or hangs back during Curculio's short monologue; see Gellar-Goad (forthcoming c) for my argument that he stays the whole time. I assume that Curculio participates in the final scenes of the play, but this is not unambiguously clear: because of questions in the textual tradition, many editions of *Curculio* have the title character not speaking, perhaps not even on stage, at the end of the play, which, indeed, would not be unusual for a Plautine comedy. But I follow the line assignments of Lanciotti (2008), who does give Curculio speaking parts, as does de Melo (2011); Lowe (2011) argues for an even larger role for Curculio in these lines.

Chapter 6

Slater (1985) is the founding father of scholarship on metatheater in Plautus; Bungard (2020) is an introductory essay to the topic. My typology of metatheater originally appeared as Gellar-Goad (2019) in the North Carolina Junior Classical League's newsletter, *The Torch*, edited by Haylie Paulin, oversight by Danetta Genung.

Fontaine (2010: 72–7) explains the *incomitiare*/*inforare* sex joke that Lyco makes at Curculio's expense. If you can read Italian, you can find a scholarly debate about the witness-summons sequence in Tandoi (1961) and Paratore (1962); I offer my own take (in English) at Gellar-Goad (forthcoming b). Duncan (2006: 113–14) argues that Curculio himself is a figure for the actor and for Roman anxieties about actors.

Chapter 7

For my discussion of the speech of the Choragus, I have found particularly useful the work of Moore (1998b: 131–9); Sommella (2005), in Italian; Marshall (2006: 40–3, 197); Suárez (2010), in Spanish; and Hanses (2020a). I build on their findings throughout this chapter.

The idea that the Choragus' speech parodies didactic poetry was put forth by Kruschwitz (2005: 127–8). I draw my comments on the profession of choragus from Marshall (2006: 26–9). Moore (2005: 32–4) advances the notion that the Choragus may have already been on stage, dressed as a silent character enslaved in Phaedromus' household. The structural parallels between Curculio and the Choragus are noted by Kruschwitz, Mulberger, and Schumacher (2001).

Richlin (2017: 380) emphasizes how rare it is for the Choragus to mention a real-life person. Welch (2003) argues that the Basilica or Atrium Regium mentioned by the Choragus was a reception hall for Greek kings, distinct from the commercial (and then judicial) functions of the later basilicas. Bettini (2015: 129) points out the connections between the Vicus Tuscus and the god Vertumnus. "Forum Plautinum":

Suárez (2010: 56–7). Richlin (2006: 61) calls attention to the recurrence of sex-laborers in the Choragus' speech.

Chapter 8

The three major studies of Plautus and enslavement are Richlin (2017), Stewart (2012), and McCarthy (2000). Richlin (2020) and Stewart (2020) offer new takes for general readers. On Plautus, sex-labor, and sex-trafficking, see Witzke (2015a), James (2010), and Marshall (2013); for an accessible entry point on the topic, read Witzke (2020). On parasites in ancient comedy, the definitive works are Tylawsky (2002) and Damon (1998).

Long after Plautus, actors would have the formal, legal low status of *infamia*. But one way to understand the Roman historian Livy's comments about the early actors of Atellan farce (7.2.12) is that actors were low status and scorned. Brown (2002: 225) remarks that: "it is likely that *infamia* developed formally out of longstanding informal prejudices." I'm not claiming legal *infamia* for actors in Plautus' time, merely low status and scorn.

Religion in Plautus is an up-and-coming area of scholarly inquiry, long overlooked; start with Jeppesen (2020), and from there consult Slater (2011), Fulkerson (2018), and Gellar-Goad (2008, 2011–12, 2013). On religion in Roman daily life, see Flower (2017). Feeney (1998: 85) discusses the Roman and Plautine practice of divine personification of abstract concepts. The point about the gendered pattern for divine oaths comes from Adams (1984). I argue the case for Cappadox as a pious sex-trafficker more extensively in Gellar-Goad (2016).

Chapter 9

On Varro's allusions in his "Bimarcus" to Plautine plays, see Gellar-Goad (2018). Catullus: Polt (2020, forthcoming); thanks to Chris for sharing a pre-publication version of his book with me. On the literary afterlife of Plautus and Terence, see Hanses (2020b, forthcoming). On improvisation in Plautus, see Slater (1993) and Marshall (2006: 245–79).

I was introduced to monks' complaints in the margins of manuscripts by Angland (2014). The data on manuscripts of Vergil and Plautus comes from Reynolds (1983). For the *editio princeps* and early critical editions of Plautus, see Ferri (2020: 414–16).

For performances of *Curculio*, the website of the Archive of Performances of Greek & Roman Drama is invaluable, at: http://www.apgrd.ox.ac.uk/. Their physical holdings underpin my comments on performances at Wellesley, Rugby, the Virginia Governor's Latin Academy, St. Olaf, Dorchester, and Mérida. The details of Guarino/Guarini's translation and performances come from Bertoni (1903: 131) and Coppo (1968: 33), and I'm indebted to Metello Mugnai for help with the translation of the quote from Guarino/Guarini's letter. Gray (1902: 94), Boas (1914: 18), and Smith (1988: 138) attest to the Jesus College, Oxford University, performance of *Curculio*. I take the point on early English translations of Plautus from Franko (2020: 446).

On Ligurio in *commedia dell'arte* and Plautine models, see Schironi (2013). On Piccolomini's *Chrysis*, Liu (2018). On Massinger and Fletcher's *A Very Woman* and *Curculio*, Gill (1967: 144). On Jonson's *The Alchemist* and *Curculio*, Cervo (1997: 128). Northrop Frye believed *Curculio* inspired the name of the trickster Brainworm in Jonson's *Every Man in His Humour*: see Dolzani (2006: 181). My source for the Moryson quote is Pritchard (2010: 6). On Chapman's *The Gentleman Usher* and *Curculio*, see Franko (2020: 453–4). On Cecchi's *I rivali* and *Curculio*, Corrigan (1958: 80). On Lenz' *Die Türkensklavin* and *Curculio*, Kes-Costa (1993: 165–72) and McInnes (1994). The anti-Semitic graphic novel is van Tilburg (2008), brought to my attention by John Oksanish.

The publication of *A Funny Thing Happened on the Way to the Forum* is Shevelove and Gelbart (1991). On countercultural aspects of *Funny Thing*, see Cull (2001: 180). On its connection to New York Jewish stand-up, Malamud (2001).

Daniela Urbanová kindly shared with me video of the Masaryk University performance of *Curculio* (at: https://medial.phil.muni.cz/Player/3492) and authorized reproduction of the photograph of Footnote. For the Virginia Governor's Latin Academy performances of *Curculio*, I am thankful for observations in personal correspondence from George Fredric Franko, Bartolo Natoli, Brent Cavedo, Nikki Carroll, Emily Jusino, and John Henkel. Same goes to Anne H. Groton for the St. Olaf performances, C. W. Marshall for the Trent University production, and Seth Jeppesen for the BYU performance. Jeppesen's BYU production is on YouTube, at https://www.youtube.com/watch?v=RLLPmdamiEk, as is the Chiclana production, at https://www.youtube.com/watch?v=AcIJLLi2El8. I am grateful also to John H. Starks for telling me about a 1991 performance of Curculio at the University of North Carolina-Chapel Hill, which I discuss in detail at Gellar-Goad (forthcoming d).

Works Cited

Adams, J. N. 1984. "Female Speech in Latin Comedy." *Antichthon* 18: 43–77.

André, Jean-Marie. 1983. "L'argent chez Plaute. Autour du *Curculio*." *Vichiana* 12: 15–35.

Andreau, J. 1968. "Banque grecque et banque romaine dans le théâtre de Plaute et de Terence." *Mélanges de l'école française de Rome* 80: 461–526.

Angland, Shane. 2014. "Massive Scribal Hangovers: One Ninth Century Confession." *Anglandicus*. Available at: http://anglandicus.blogspot.com/2014/12/massive-scribal-hangovers-one-ninth.html.

Augello, Giuseppe. 1983. "Il ditirambo di Leonessa al vino nel *Curculio* (vv. 96–109)." *Dioniso* 54: 247–53.

Bertoni, Gilio. 1903. *La Biblioteca Estense e la coltura ferrarese ai tempi del Duca I (1471–1505)*. Turin.

Bettini, Maurizio. 2015. *Il dio elegante. Vertumno e la religione romana*. Turin.

Boas, Frederick S. 1914. *University Drama in the Tudor Age*. Oxford.

Bond, Sarah E. 2017. "Why We Need to Start Seeing the Classical World in Color." *Hyperallergic*. Available at: https://hyperallergic.com/383776/why-we-need-to-start-seeing-the-classical-world-in-color/.

Brown, P. G. M. 2002. "Actors and Actor-Managers at Rome in the Time of Plautus and Terence." In Pat Easterling and Edith Hall, eds. *Greek and Roman Actors: Aspects of an Ancient Profession*. Cambridge. 225–37.

Bungard, Christopher. 2020. "Metatheater and Improvisation in Plautus." In Dorota Dutsch and George Fredric Franko, eds. *A Companion to Plautus*. Malden, MA. 237–50.

Burton, Paul J. 2020. "Warfare and Imperialism in and Around Plautus." In Dorota Dutsch and George Fredric Franko, eds. *A Companion to Plautus*. Malden, MA. 301–16.

Cervo, Nathan. 1997. "Jonson's *The Alchemist*." *Explicator* 55.3: 128–9.

Cohen, Amy R. 2007. "Can You Hear Me Now?—Implications of New Research in Greek Theatrical Masks." *Didaskalia* 7.1. Available at: https://www.didaskalia.net/issues/vol7no1/cohen.html.

Conte, Gian Biagio. 1999. *Latin Literature: A History*. Joseph B. Solodow, trans., rev. Don P. Fowler and Glenn W. Most. Baltimore, MD.

Coppo, Anna Maria. 1968. "Spettacoli alla corte di Ercole I." *Contributi dell'Istituto di Filologia Moderna: Pubblicazioni dell'Università Cattolica del Sacro Cuore: Serie Storia del teatro* 1: 30–59.

Corrigan, Beatrice M. 1958. "*Il Capriccio*: An Unpublished Italian Renaissance Comedy and Its Analogues." *Studies in the Renaissance* 5: 74–86.

Cull, Nicholas J. 2001. "'Infamy! Infamy! They've All Got It in for Me!': *Carry On Cleo* and the British Camp Comedies of Ancient Rome." In Sandra R. Joshel, Margaret Malamud, and Donald T. McGuire, eds. *Imperial Projections: Ancient Rome in Modern Popular Culture*. Baltimore, MD. 162–90.

Damen, Mark. 2012. "Roman Comedy, Part 1 (Plautus)." Classical Drama and Society course website. Available at: https://www.usu.edu/markdamen/ClasDram/chapters/141plautus.htm.

Damon, Cynthia. 1998. *The Mask of the Parasite: A Pathology of Roman Patronage*. Ann Arbor, MI.

de Melo, Wolfgang, trans. 2011. *Plautus. Casina; The Casket Comedy; Curculio; Epidicus; The Two Menaechmuses*. Cambridge, MA.

Dolzani, Michael, ed. 2006. *Northrop Frye's Notebooks on Renaissance Literature*, vol. 20. Toronto.

Duckworth, George E. 1952. *The Nature of Roman Comedy: A Study in Popular Entertainment*. Princeton, NJ.

Duncan, Anne. 2006. Performance and Identity in the Classical World. Cambridge.

Dutsch, Dorota and George Fredric Franko, eds. 2020. *A Companion to Plautus*. Malden, MA.

Fantham, Elaine. 1965. "The *Curculio* of Plautus: An Illustration of Plautine Methods in Adaptation." *Classical Quarterly* 15: 84–100.

Fantham, Elaine. 1991. "*Stuprum*: Public Attitudes and Penalties for Sexual Offences in Republican Rome." *Échos du monde classique* 35.3: 267–91.

Feeney, Denis. 1998. *Literature and Religion at Rome: Cultures, Contexts, and Beliefs*. Cambridge.

Ferri, Rolando. 2020. "The Textual Tradition of Plautus." In Dorota Dutsch and George Fredric Franko, eds. *A Companion to Plautus*. Malden, MA. 407–18.

Flower, Harriet I. 2017. *The Dancing Lares and the Serpent in the Garden: Religion at the Roman Street Corner*. Princeton, NJ.

Fontaine, Michael. 2010. *Funny Words in Plautine Comedy*. Oxford.

Fraenkel, Eduard. 2007. *Plautine Elements in Plautus*. Frances Muecke and Tomas Drevikovsky, trans. Oxford.

Franko, George Fredric. 2020. "Plautus in Early Modern England." In Dorota Dutsch and George Fredric Franko, eds. *A Companion to Plautus*. Malden, MA. 445–59.

Fulkerson, Laurel. 2018. "*Deos speravi* (*Miles* 1209): Hope and the Gods in Roman Comedy." In George Kazantzidis and Dimos Sparathas, eds. *Hope in Ancient Literature, History, and Art*. Berlin. 153–70.

Gellar-Goad, T. H. M. 2008. "Sacrifice and Ritual Imagery in Menander, Plautus, and Terence." MA thesis, University of North Carolina at Chapel Hill.

Gellar-Goad, T. H. M. 2011–12. "The *Seruus Callidus* and Ritual Imagery in Plautus' *Epidicus*." *Classical Journal* 107.2: 149–64.

Gellar-Goad, T. H. M. 2013. "Religious Ritual and Family Dynamics in Terence." In Antony Augoustakis and Ariana Traill, eds. *A Companion to Terence*. Malden, MA. 156–74.

Gellar-Goad, T. H. M. 2014. Review of Moore 2012a. *Bryn Mawr Classical Review* 2014.08.46. Available at: http://bmcr.brynmawr.edu/2014/2014-08-46.html.

Gellar-Goad, T. H. M. 2016. "Plautus' *Curculio* and the Case of the Pious Pimp." In Stavros Frangoulidis, Stephen J. Harrison, and Gesine Manuwald, eds. *Roman Drama and Its Contexts*. Berlin. 231–52.

Gellar-Goad, T. H. M. 2018. "Varro's *Bimarcus* and Encounters with the Self in Plautus's *Epidicus* and *Amphitruo*." *Arethusa* 51.2: 117–35.

Gellar-Goad, T. H. M. 2019. "'Meta' Matters in Ancient Comedy." *The Torch* 2: 5.

Gellar-Goad, T. H. M. 2020. "Music and Meter in Plautus." In Dorota Dutsch and George Fredric Franko, eds. *A Companion to Plautus*. Malden, MA. 251–68.

Gellar-Goad, T. H. M. Forthcoming a. "Amore o lavoro? Planesio la (*pseudo*?)-*meretrix* del *Curculio* e le esigenze del meretricio." In Giorgia Bandini and Caterina Pentericci, eds. *Personaggi in scena: la* meretrix. Rome. 23–32.

Gellar-Goad, T. H. M. Forthcoming b. "*Antestari*: Procedural Law in *Curculio* 620–625." *Philologus*.

Gellar-Goad, T. H. M. Forthcoming c. "Therapontigonus Was on Stage the Whole Time: A Note on Stagecraft in Plautus' *Curculio*." *Mnemosyne*.

Gellar-Goad, T. H. M. Forthcoming d. A Commentary on Plautus' Curculio. Ann Arbor.

Giangreco Passi, Maria Vittoria. 1981. "*Argentarii* e *trapeziti* nel teatro di Plauto." *Archivio giuridico Filippo Serafini* 201: 39–106.

Gill, Roma. 1967. "Collaboration and Revision in Massinger's *A Very Woman*." *Review of English Studies* 18.70: 136–48.

Gitner, Adam. 2016. "*Nautea, notia*: A Nauseating Root in Plautus." *Glotta* 92: 110–30.

Gratwick, Adrian S. 1982. "Drama." In E. J. Kenney and W. V. Clausen, eds. *The Cambridge History of Classical Literature*, vol. 2. Cambridge. 77–137.

Gray, Arthur. 1902. *Jesus College*. London.

Habinek, Thomas. 2005. *The World of Roman Song: From Ritualized Speech to Social Order*. Baltimore, MD.

Hanses, Mathias. 2020a (forthcoming). "Men among Monuments: Roman Memory and Roman Topography in Plautus's *Curculio*." *Classical Philology* 115.4: 630–58.

Hanses, Mathias. 2020b (forthcoming). *The Life of Comedy after the Death of Plautus and Terence*. Ann Arbor, MI.

Hornblower, Simon, Antony Spawnforth, and Esther Eidinow, eds. 2012. *The Oxford Classical Dictionary*. 4th edn. Oxford: Oxford University Press.

James, Sharon L. 2010. "Trafficking Pasicompsa: A Courtesan's Travels and Travails in Plautus' *Mercator*." *New England Classical Journal* 37: 39–50.

James, Sharon L. 2020. "Plautus and the Marriage Plot." In Dorota Dutsch and George Fredric Franko, eds. *A Companion to Plautus*. Malden, MA. 109–22.

Jeppesen, Seth A. 2020. "Religion in and Around Plautus." In Dorota Dutsch and George Fredric Franko, eds. *A Companion to Plautus*. Malden, MA. 317–30.

Joshel, Sandra R., Margaret Malamud, and Donald T. McGuire, eds. 2001. *Imperial Projections: Ancient Rome in Modern Popular Culture*. Baltimore, MD.

Kes-Costa, Barbara R. 1993. "'Freundschaft geht über Natur': On Lenz's Rediscovered Adaptation of Plautus." In Alan C. Leidner and Helga Stipa Madland, eds. *Space to Act: The Theater of J. M. R. Lenz*. Columbia, SC. 162–73.

Ketterer, Robert C. 1986. "Stage properties in Plautine comedy I." *Semiotica* 58.3–4: 193–216.

Kruschwitz, Peter. 2005. "Lehre oder Dichtung? Die archaische didaktische Poesie der Römer." In Marietta Horster and Christiane Reitz, eds. *Wissensvermittlung in dichterischer Gestalt*. Stuttgart. 115–31.

Kruschwitz, Peter, J. Mulberger, and M. Schumacher. 2001. "Die Struktur des 'Curculio.'" *Gymnasium* 108.2: 113–21.

Lanciotti, Settimio, ed. 2008. *Titus Maccius Plautus. Curculio*. Sarsina.

Lefèvre, Eckard. 1991. "Curculio oder Der Triumph der Edazität." In Eckard Lefèvre, Ekkehard Stärk, and Gregor Vogt-Spira, eds. Plautus barbarus: *Sechs Kapitel zur Originalität des Plautus*. Tübingen. 71–105.

Leigh, Matthew. 2004. *Comedy and the Rise of Rome*. Oxford.

Liu, Cynthia C. 2018. "*Chrysis*: Text, Translation, and Commentary of Enea Silvio Piccolomini's Latin comedy." BA Honors thesis, Baylor University, Waco, TX.

Lowe, J. C. B. 2011. "The Finale of Plautus' *Curculio*." *Rheinisches Museum* 154.3–4: 285–99.

Ludwig, Walther. 1967. "Ein plautinisches Canticum. *Curculio* 96–157." *Philologus* 111: 186–97.

Malamud, Margaret. 2001. "Brooklyn-on-the-Tiber: Roman Comedy on Broadway and in Film." In Sandra R. Joshel, Margaret Malamud, and Donald T. McGuire, eds. *Imperial Projections: Ancient Rome in Modern Popular Culture*. Baltimore, MD. 191–208.

Marshall, C. W. 2006. *The Stagecraft and Performance of Roman Comedy*. Cambridge.

Marshall, C. W. 2013. "Sex slaves in New Comedy." In Ben Akrigg and Rob Tordoff, eds. *Slaves and Slavery in Ancient Greek Comic Drama*. Cambridge. 173–196.

McCarthy, Kathleen. 2000. *Slaves, Masters and the Art of Authority in Plautine Comedy*. Princeton, NJ.

McCoskey, Denise Eileen. 2012. *Race: Antiquity and Its Legacy*. Oxford.

McInnes, Edward. 1994. "Lenz, Shakespeare, Plautus and the 'Unlaughing Picture.'" In David Hill, ed. *Jakob Michael Reinhold Lenz: Studien zum Gesamtwerk*. Opladen. 27–35.

Moore, Timothy J. 1998a. "Music and Structure in Roman Comedy." *American Journal of Philology* 119.2: 245–73.

Moore, Timothy J. 1998b. *The Theatre of Plautus: Playing to the Audience*. Austin, TX.

Moore, Timothy J. 2005. "*Pessuli, heus pessuli*: La porta nel *Curculio*." Renato Raffaelli and Alba Tontini, eds. *Curculio (Sarsina, 25 settembre 2004)*. Urbino. 11–36.

Moore, Timothy J. 2012a. *Music in Roman Comedy*. Oxford.

Moore, Timothy J. 2012b. *Roman Theatre*. Cambridge.

Moore, Timothy J. 2012–13. "Don't Skip the Meter! Introducing Students to the Music of Roman Comedy." *Classical Journal* 108: 218–34.

Papaioannou, Sophia. 2008/2009. "What's in a Name? The Real Identity of Palinurus in Plautus' *Curculio*." *Classical Journal* 104.2: 111–22.

Paratore, Ettore. 1962. "Antestor nel *Curculio* e nel *Poenulus*." *Dioniso* 36: 98–122.

Philippides, Katerina. 2018. "Sickness and Cure in Plautus' *Curculio*." *Mnemosyne* 71.2: 281–97.

Pieczonka, Joanna. 2019. "Stock Characters from *Atellana* in Plautus' *Palliata* – The Connections between *Dossennus-Manducus* and the Plautine Parasites Reconsidered." *Graeco-Latina Brunensia* 24.2: 193–210.

Polt, Christopher B. 2020 (forthcoming). *Catullus and Roman Comedy: Performance, Tradition, and Personal Drama*. Cambridge.

Pritchard, R. E., ed. 2010. *Shakespeare's England: Life in Elizabethan & Jacobean Times*. Stroud, Gloucestershire.

Questa, Cesare. 1995. *Titi Macci Plauti Cantica*. Urbino.

Radif, Ludovica. 2005. "Il *bellum Sapphicum* nel *Curculio*." *Maia* 57.1: 19–23.

Raffaelli, Renato and Alba Tontini, eds. 2005. *Curculio (Sarsina, 25 settembre 2004)*. Urbino.

Reynolds, L. D., ed. 1983. *Texts and Transmission: A Survey of the Latin Classics*. Oxford.

Richlin, Amy, trans. 2006. *Rome and the Mysterious Orient: Three Plays by Plautus*. Berkeley, CA.

Richlin, Amy. 2017. *Slave Theater in the Roman Republic: Plautus and Popular Comedy*. Cambridge.

Richlin, Amy. 2020. "Owners and Slaves in and Around Plautus." In Dorota Dutsch and George Fredric Franko, eds. *A Companion to Plautus*. Malden, MA. 347–60.

Scafuro, Adele C. 1997. *The Forensic Stage: Settling Disputes in Graeco-Roman New Comedy*. Cambridge.

Schironi, Francesca. 2013. "The Trickster Onstage: The Cunning Slave from Plautus to Commedia dell'Arte." In S. Douglas Olson, ed. *Ancient Comedy and Reception: Essays in Honor of Jeffrey Henderson*. Berlin. 447–78.

Segal, Erich. 1968. *Roman Laughter: The Comedy of Plautus*. Cambridge, MA.

Sharrock, Alison. 2008. "The Theatrical Life of Things: Plautus and the Physical." *Dictynna* 5. Available at: http://journals.openedition.org/dictynna/419.

Shelton, Jo-Ann, ed. 1997. *As the Romans Did: A Sourcebook in Roman Social History*. Oxford.

Shevelove, Burt and Larry Gelbart. 1991. *A Funny Thing Happened on the Way to the Forum*. New York.

Slater, Niall W. 1985. *Plautus in Performance: The Theatre of the Mind*. Princeton, NJ.

Slater, Niall W. 1993. "Improvisation in Plautus." In Gregor Vogt-Spira, ed. *Beiträge zur mündlichen Kultur der Römer*. Tübingen. 113–24.

Slater, Niall W. 2001. "Appearance, Reality, and the Spectre of Incest in *Epidicus*." In Ulrike Auhagen, ed. *Studien zu Plautus' Epidicus*. Tübingen. 191–203.

Slater, Niall W. 2011. "Plautus the Theologian." In André Lardinois, Josine Blok, and M. G. M. van der Poel, eds. *Sacred Words: Orality, Literacy and Religion*. Leiden. 295–310.

Smith, Bruce R. 1988. *Ancient Scripts and Modern Experience on the English Stage, 1500–1700*. Princeton, NJ.

Sommella, Paolo. 2005. "La Roma plautina (con particolare riferimento a *Cur*. 467–85)." In Renato Raffaelli and Alba Tontini, eds. *Curculio (Sarsina, 25 settembre 2004)*. Urbino. 69–106.

Stewart, Roberta. 2012. *Plautus and Roman Slavery*. Malden, MA.

Stewart, Roberta. 2020. "Slave Labor in Plautus." In Dorota Dutsch and George Fredric Franko, eds. *A Companion to Plautus*. Malden, MA. 361–78.

Suárez, Marcela Alejandra. 2010. "El monólogo del corego en '*Curculio*': un 'tour' por la memoria." *Revista de estudios latinos* 10: 49–61.

Tandoi, Vincenzo. 1961. "Un passo del *Curculio* e la semantica di *antestor*." *Studi italiani di filologia classica* 33: 62–86.

Tylawsky, Elizabeth Ivory. 2002. *Saturio's Inheritance: The Greek Ancestry of the Roman Comic Parasite*. New York.

van Tilburg, Magda. 2008. *Curculio, Plautus*. Darmstadt. Available at: https://booxalive.nl/curculiokorenwurm/.

von Antonsen-Resch, Andrea. 2005. *Von Gnathon zu Saturio. Die Parasitenfigur und das Verhältnis der römischen Komödie zur griechischen*. Berlin.

Welch, Katherine. 2003. "A New View of the Origins of the Basilica: The Atrium Regium, Graecostasis, and Roman Diplomacy." *Journal of Roman Archaeology* 16: 5–34.

Wiles, David. 1991. *The Masks of Menander: Sign and Meaning in Greek and Roman Performance*. Cambridge.

Wiseman, T. P. 1985. *Catullus and His World: A Reappraisal*. Cambridge.

Witzke, Serena S. 2015a. "Harlots, Tarts, and Hussies? A Problem of Terminology for Sex Labor in Roman Comedy." *Helios* 42.1: 7–27.

Witzke, Serena S. 2015b. "'I Went in a Lover and Came out a Brother?' Near-Miss Incest in Plautus' Comedies." Conference paper, Classical Association of the Middle West and South meeting. Boulder, CO.

Witzke, Serena S. 2020. "Gender and Sexuality in Plautus." In Dorota Dutsch and George Fredric Franko, eds. *A Companion to Plautus*. Malden, MA. 331–46.

Wright, John, ed. 1993. *Plautus Curculio*. Norman, OK.

Zuckerberg, Donna. 2018. *Not All Dead White Men: Classics and Misogyny in the Digital Age*. Cambridge, MA.

Index

Note: page numbers in **bold** refer to the tables.